A THREEFOLD CORD

A Threefold Cord

A Devotional For Couples
2nd Edition

*Though one may be overpowered,
two can defend themselves.
A cord of three strands is not quickly broken.*
—Ecclesiastes 4:12

Bill and Penny Banuchi
Marriage & Family Savers Ministries

XULON PRESS

Xulon Press
2301 Lucien Way #415
Maitland, FL 32751
407.339.4217
www.xulonpress.com

© 2020 by Bill and Penny Banuchi

All rights reserved solely by the author. The author guarantees all contents are original and do not infringe upon the legal rights of any other person or work. No part of this book may be reproduced in any form without the permission of the author. The views expressed in this book are not necessarily those of the publisher.

Unless otherwise indicated, Scripture quotations taken from the Holy Bible, New International Version (NIV). Copyright © 1973, 1978, 1984, 2011 by Biblica, Inc.™. Used by permission. All rights reserved.

Printed in the United States of America.

ISBN-13: 978-1-6305-0795-4

Dedication

We wish to dedicate this work, first of all, to Jesus Christ, the One who gave us the hope, wisdom and power to save our marriage from being included in the sad divorce statistics of our time.

Secondly, to all the saints who have helped us through, prayed us through and loved us through—even when we were quite unlovable—to see our marriage restored, and ultimately, to be used to bring healing and restoration to so many other marriages and families, all for God's glory.

And most importantly to us, we want to dedicate this book—which in many ways reflects much of our life's work—to our children, Dulcinea and Will Jr., and our grandchildren, Marina and Alejandro. It is our sincerest prayer that whatever wisdom can be gleaned from these pages is passed on to future generations, and most importantly, the understanding of the necessity for a personal relationship with Jesus Christ to effectively apply these principles.

And finally, to all the couples we've had the privilege of serving to help find restoration and healing for their marriages. Whatever we have passed on to others we have received, once again, for ourselves. One of our greatest rewards in this life has been to see God's miraculous handiwork in the marriages saved and the families we have seen restored by the power of His love. Let us all continue as has been said, "One beggar telling another beggar where to find bread." Only, it is so much more!

Table of Contents

Dedication v
Preface xiii
Foreword xvii
#1 Accepting One Another 1
#2 Affection 2
#3 A State Of Being 3
#4 A Cancer Called Anger 4
#5 Assertiveness Training 101 5
#6 Au Contraire 6
#7 Barriers to Forgiveness 7
#8 Be an Encourager 8
#9 Bigger Than Both of Us 9
#10 Communicate You Care 10
#11 A Team Sport 11
#12 An Empty Nest 12
#13 Expectations 13
#14 Eyes on the Donut 14
#15 Feelings 15
#16 Fig Leaves Don't Cover 16
#17 Fix the Problem 17
#18 Forgiveness and Forgivingness 18
#19 Fruit Inspectors 19

#20 Giving Freely 20
#21 God Is in Control 21
#22 Growing in Oneness 22
#23 Head of the House? 23
#24 Honor One Another 24
#25 Intimacy or Sex? 25
#26 In the Moment 26
#27 Hula Hoop Therapy 27
#28 Letter or Spirit? 28
#29 It's All His Anyway 29
#30 Follow Your Heart?—Not! 30
#31 Listen to Understand 31
#32 Marriage, A Sacred Trust 32
#33 Redeem the Times! 33
#34 No Jesus, No Peace 34
#35 Don't Isolate 35
#36 What Really Matters 36
#37 Road Work 37
#38 You Are an Example 38
#39 The "S" Word 39
#40 Loving Leadership 40
#41 The Power of Two 41
#42 Whose Body Is It Anyway? 42
#43 Marriage Training 43
#44 Times of Refreshing 44
#45 Relationships or Volley Balls 45
#46 Repentance...Ugh! 46
#47 Respond vs. Reacting 47

#48 Your In-House Counselor............................48
#49 The Language Of Intimacy 49
#50 The Light in You 50
#51 The Place of Peace................................51
#52 The Power of Life and Death.......................52
#53 Truth and Grace...................................53
#54 Marriage and Politics..............................54
#55 Two Are Better....................................55
#56 When We're Apart 56
#57 Who or What?.....................................57
#58 Who to Please.....................................58
#59 Why Haven't I Died Yet Lord? 59
#60 You Have an Enemy................................60
#61 Are We Ready?....................................61
#62 An Overcomer or a "Hanger-Inner?"..................62
#63 Love Compels 63
#64 Real Climate Change...............................64
#65 Cockles of Your Heart 65
#66 Strife Eliminator...................................66
#67 What Drives You, Faith or Fear? 67
#68 Straining Forward 68
#69 When Bad Things Happen..........................69
#70 Learning to Love 70
#71 Q-Tip Therapy 71
#72 Change 72
#73 Grateful or Grumbler?..............................73
#74 The Liberty of Love................................74
75 When It's Mathematically Impossible!................75

#76 Let's Talk Adult-to-Adult........................... 76
#77 Break the Curse 79
#78 Not Fake News....................................... 80
#79 How Joseph Loved Mary............................ 81
#80 Wise Couples Still Seek Him........................ 82
#81 Christmas and Marriage............................. 83
#82 Rejoice With Truth (New Years) 84
#83 New Year's "Repentolutions" 85
#84 Vision For the New Year 86
#85 Valentine's Day and Marriage 87
#86 Prepare For the Storm 89
#87 Through the Storm.................................. 90
#88 After the Storm..................................... 91
#89 An Interesting Fast (Lent) 92
#90 Resurrection and Marriage.......................... 93
#91 Spring Clean Up..................................... 94
#92 Mother's Day 95
#93 Why Remember? (Memorial Day) 96
#94 Father's Day.. 98
#95 Her Perspective on Father's Day 99
#96 Freedom 100
#97 Oh Holy Vacation................................... 101
#98 What are Vacations For? 102
#99 Changing Seasons 104
#100 For Him (Election Day)............................ 105
#101 A Grateful Heart................................... 106
#102 Thanksgiving –It's Fundamental 107
#103 Love Is Patient.................................... 109

#104 Love Is Kind 110
#105 Love Does Not Envy 111
#106 Love Does Not Boast! 112
#107 Love Is Not Proud 113
#108 Love Is Not Rude 114
#109 Love Is Not Self-Seeking 115
#110 Love Is Not Easily Angered 116
#111 Love Keeps No Record of Wrongs 117
#112 Love Doesn't Delight In Evil 118
#113 Rejoices With Truth 119
#114 Love Always Protects 120
#115 Love Always Trusts 121
#116 Love Always Hopes 122
#117 Love Always Perseveres 123
#118 Love Never Fails 124
Our Marriage Journal 128

Preface

These devotionals originated on our website as a way to minister to couples beyond our physical reach. It soon became apparent to us that God was using them to bring healing and restoration to more couples than we ever could have imagined.

So, the next step seemed to be to put them all together in one book to reach even more couples. This edition is an expanded version of the first book published in 2003. It is, in effect, an extension of our seminars and counseling ministry.

These devotionals incorporate many of the principles that we have been using for more than twenty years in our ministry to couples. These principles have helped to save troubled marriages, enrich healthy marriages and prepare couples to enter into marriage with tools for success. In that time, we have seen the restoration of marriages that initially appeared impossible to save, but yet with a couples' willingness, and God's power, individuals are saved, marriages are healed, families are restored and God gets the glory!

You see, we were on the brink of divorce in our twentieth year of marriage. We had three teenagers at home, and we were in the pastorate at this point for more than eight years. But rather than give in to the current trend to divorce, we chose to work through our crisis which called for addressing complex issues that had been left unaddressed for twenty years. It was difficult, but it was so worth it. Today, married for more than fifty years, we can honestly say we are more in love than we were when we were married at eighteen and nineteen years old.

So, these devotionals are not only the product of professional education and training, but we believe, more importantly, they are the product of the time-tested application of these principles in our own experience. In fact, the very reason why this ministry was birthed was simply to pass on to others what God has done for us, for we know, as the Scriptures say, God is no respecter of persons. What he did for Bill and Penny He will do for whosoever would submit to His design for marriage and family.

We encourage couples to approach theses devotionals diligently and prayerfully. They can truly become an instrument of healing and restoration. They may prompt you to seek professional counseling. If they do, be sure the counseling you seek is truly Christian. Secular counselors often counsel from a different worldview that places personal happiness as the goal. A Christian worldview sees happiness, not as the goal of life, but rather, as the result of a life lived in the pursuit of God's plan—*it works!*

The title of each devotional will give you an idea of the subject addressed. You'll find a relevant verse of Scripture at the top of each page, and then our thoughts concerning the subject. Most importantly, at the end of each devotional you'll find a question to prompt dialogue, and a prayer starter to help train each couple to pray together.

Find a quiet place and time to share these devotionals together. Commit yourselves to "working" to see your marriage become all God wants it to be for the benefit of the children, your happiness and ultimately, for God's glory.

In the back of the book we have reserved space for you to record what God is showing you about your marriage journey in a section entitled "Our Marriage Journal." Make entries into it as God gives you revelation.

We serve a God of miracles. We have seen them. We have experienced them. You too, can have a testimony of a marriage saved, a

Preface

family restored, and yes, it will be work, but it will be so worth it. And God will get the glory!

Please feel free to e-mail your comments or questions to **info@marriageandfamily.org**.

Foreword

In a day when families and marriages face challenges as never before, this devotional book provides encouragement for couples to bring every thought, feeling and action into the light of God's truth and love. It is a must for every home!

Bill and Penny have a passion, and a desire to bring unity and wholeness into the lives of couples, marriages and families. They have brought insight to Scripture revealed to them as they strained forward, grappling with circumstances and stresses together as they sought to find balance in their own lives. They present questions that will provoke meaningful times of communication. These insights will help couples and families to stand on the solid rock of the Word of God, our only sure foundation in an unsure world.

Inspiring, and encouraging, these practical devotionals draw us closer to God while strengthening our relationships with one another.

Dr. J. Patrick Fiore
Christian Life Center

#1 Accepting One Another

> *"Accept one another, then, just as Christ accepted you, in order to bring praise to God."* —Romans 15:7

Can we accept one another just as we are, without thinking that one is better than the other? The Bible teaches that there is no difference. You see, the law cannot be kept in part. Once a law is broken, the individual is counted guilty for breaking every law in the Book. (James 2:10). Therefore both husband and wife are equally guilty, but Praise God, they are also equally forgiven in Christ! That's why it's been said that the ground is level at the cross. No one can stand taller than the other.

We need to accept one another, not for what we are, because we all fall short, but for who we are–God's gift to one another. If God were to extend his arm down through the clouds, and say, "Here, I have a gift for you." He opens his hand and there you see a piece of coal. What would you do with that gift? Would you discard it? Treat it irreverently, because it's only a piece of coal? Or would you value it highly because of who gave you the gift? So it is with your spouse. He or she is not to be valued for what they are, but for who they are —*God's gift to you.* You may see a piece of coal, but God sees a diamond in the making, no different than yourself.

So let's make a decision today to accept one another, just as Christ accepts us, not for what we are, but for who we are- God's gift to one another -diamonds in the making!

Question for Dialogue: Can you truly see me as God's gift to you? Are there certain things about me you find difficult to accept?

Pray Together: Lord, help us to see each other as your gift to us. Help us to accept one another just as we are, as we both struggle to change every day.

#2 Affection

"It is right for me to feel this way about all of you, since I have you in my heart… God can testify how I long for all of you with the affection of Christ Jesus." —Philippians 1:7,8

Paul is saying a whole lot here. He seems to be encouraging believers, (That's you I hope), to be tenderhearted and kind to one another as we struggle to change day by day. He seems to be saying, "Don't sweat the small stuff. God will take care of it. He will finish the work and set everybody straight. Don't worry about it. Just give yourselves to treating one another with kindness and affection." He's encouraging us to look past the faults. Be ministers of grace. Enjoy the journey. There's no better way to share life's journey than with heart-felt affection —the affection of Christ Jesus.

It begins with the look in your eye. Do your eyes communicate affection? Try this: Before you speak to your spouse, think: "I love you." The very spirit of love will come through in the gleam in your eye. Your tone of voice will communicate affection. More important than the words you use, is the spirit behind the words. Let your words be affectionate. How about an affectionate non-sexual physical touch? Yes, it must be non-sexual if it's to communicate affection. A touch on the cheek, a stroke on one's shoulder. Whatever form it takes affection says, "I love you. I care for you. I highly desire you. You are special to me." Take the time and make the effort to understand what forms of affection truly minister grace to your spouse. Then give yourself to the challenge.

Question for Dialogue: If there was such a thing as an "affection-ometer" for our marriage what would it show?

Pray Together: Lord, help us to be tender-hearted and kind to one another, and to demonstrate an affection toward one another that says, "I love and appreciate you dearly."

#3 A State Of Being

"Be kind and compassionate to one another, forgiving each other, just as in Christ God forgave you." —Ephesians 4:32

Paul isn't talking about something we should be doing. He's talking about a state of being, a state of continually receiving God's forgiveness through Christ, and being a vessel through which forgiveness passes to another. It's a dynamic thing. As you are being forgiven, you allow the flow of grace to pass through you into the lives of others. When you are offended you forgive, because you are in a state of being a channel of forgiveness. Even while you are being offended, you are "being" forgiving. You're not waiting for your spouse to say, "I'm sorry." You are already giving forgiveness because this is who you are. You are being kind, compassionate and forgiving. Aren't you glad Jesus didn't wait for you to say you were sorry before He hung on the cross for you? He didn't say, "I'll hang on this cross if you'll repent." He just hung, and offered himself willingly to "whosoever will". Our love and devotion to Him is a response to that unconditional love and forgiveness He demonstrated. Our spouses' love and devotion to us will also be a response to the unconditional love we demonstrate as we are being kind and compassionate, forgiving each other. It's not what you do; it's who you are being.

Question for Dialogue: When do we each feel that we're not being forgiving to one another?

Pray Together: Lord, help us to remain in the flow of your grace so that we can be forgiving of one another even as you are forgiving of us.

#4 A Cancer Called Anger

"Better a patient man than a warrior, a man who controls his temper than one who takes a city." — Proverbs 16:32

Nothing is more devastating to a relationship than residual anger that continually pops up its ugly head at the slightest provocation. An angry person is incapable of having a healthy loving relationship with anyone. Now, we all get angry from time to time. That's not the problem. Even Jesus got angry, but in his expression of anger he didn't sin. The anger isn't the problem. It's how we express it that can get us into trouble. If we don't express it properly it can be destructive. If we keep stuffing it, eventually it will find its way into every cell of our being until we become an angry person. In other words, it's one thing to be a person who gets angry from time to time. It's another thing to be an angry person. An angry person is incapable of a healthy loving relationship. Unresolved anger becomes a barrier to intimacy. It's no longer just a temporary feeling; it becomes part of who you are. Unresolved anger is a marriage and family killer. We need to be honest with ourselves. Take inventory to determine if you have residual anger toward anyone, or anything, or even God! Then work toward repentance and forgiveness until the cancer of anger is fully removed and replaced with God's tenderness and mercy. Then you will be able to receive God's love for yourself, and extend it to others, or the cancer called anger will continue on it's course of destruction.

Question for Dialogue: How do we each handle our anger? Do we have angry outbursts or do we just stuff it? Do we have any residual anger from our past?

Pray Together: Lord, help us to manage our anger in a way that is pleasing to you. Help us to replace it with your tenderness and mercy.

#5 Assertiveness Training 101

> *"Surely, you desire truth in the innermost parts"*
> —Psalm 51:6

Assertiveness is one of the most important factors affecting our relationships. Too often, our desire to keep the peace causes us to sacrifice truth, because we're afraid of "rocking the boat." Whenever we sacrifice truth in this way we can be certain it will cause a problem, if not today, then in the future. It will show up in the form of resentment, bitterness or strife. When we don't express how we truly feel about an issue we send a message by our silence that is not reflective of who we really are, and how we really feel. Therefore, our spouse gets a false impression. You may have peace for now but that peace is based on less than a truthful representation of who you are and how you feel. Your partner cannot come to know you until you decide to speak the truth in love. This assertiveness is essential for a growing, healthy relationship. This is what God desires from us, "truth in the innermost parts," and this is what we must give one another, even when it means some discomfort. Yes, we need to use wisdom and sensitivity concerning timing, but we do need to share truthfully. This is the foundation of healthy communication.

Question for Dialogue: What are some of the important issues we don't talk about just to keep the peace?

Pray Together: Lord, help us to be courageous enough to speak the truth in love with each other, yet with the wisdom and timing of the Holy Spirit.

#6 Au Contraire

"Can two walk together, except they be agreed?"
—Amos 3:3 (KJV)

Too many couples have communication problems because at least one party – sometimes both- has a contrary spirit. No, I don't mean they are possessed by a demon, but there is an inner default mechanism programmed to counter whatever the other spouse says. We hear it all the time in the counseling room, "I say black; you say white." Sometimes we observe one spouse just sitting, watching and waiting for something they can pounce on to contradict or challenge. Regardless of whether or not there is merit to the contradiction, the result is that the parties will be in opposition to each other instead of being "one." If there's going to be any meaningful, mutually edifying communication, it must begin with both parties feeling they are on the same side, straining forward together, as one. Establishing that oneness provides the atmosphere of grace that makes it possible to communicate. Even if you disagree with your spouse, you can still find something to agree about first to establish that emotional unity, and from that place you can express your thoughts and opinions speaking the truth in love. In any event, choose to find a point of agreement first instead of reacting negatively. Don't let that contrary spirit shut down communication and intimacy.

Question for Dialogue: Do you think I have a contrary spirit? Does it cause you to hesitate to share things with me?

Pray Together: Lord, help us to think *first* of what we agree on, so that we will feel we're on the same team. Help us to no longer give in to a contrary spirit.

#7 Barriers to Forgiveness

"For if you forgive men when they sin against you, your heavenly Father will also forgive you. But if you do not forgive men their sins, your father will not forgive your sins."
—Matt. 6:14,15

When our spouse hurts us, especially over a period of time, we tend to see them no longer as our spouse but as "the one who is hurting me." We subconsciously see ourselves in an adversarial relationship as though our spouse were the enemy against whom we must protect. The first step in forgiving (so that we may be forgiven) is to see your spouse not as the one who is hurting you out of a desire to do you ill, but as one who has hurt you because he or she is a hurt, flawed, weak human being, just like you, struggling to change day by day. Remember, hurting people hurt other people. Your spouse hurt you, because their history, or their lack of relationship with Christ, hasn't taught them how to forgive or how to love. This is particularly true if your spouse doesn't know God. The Bible tells us that unless someone knows God they simply cannot know love because God is love. Let's begin to see one another as God sees us – as flawed weak human beings who hurt one another out of our own hurts. Let's begin to forgive, because, we too, need forgiveness to keep the flow of God's grace unrestricted and freely flowing in and through our hearts to touch the hearts of others.

Question for Dialogue: Do you see me as the one who is hurting you, or as a flawed human being, struggling to change?

Pray Together: Dear Lord, help us to see one another as you see us, as flawed believers learning to love and growing day by day.

#8 BE AN ENCOURAGER

"Therefore encourage one another and build each other up, as you are doing." —I Thessalonians. 5:11

There may be days when we just want the world to go away. We would rather stay in bed and pull the covers up over our heads than have to deal with life. Thank God Jesus didn't take that attitude. He knew full well in those last days that he would be betrayed, denied three times by one of his closest friends and then crucified, (Talk about a reason to get the blues!) Yet, he would still press on because of his commitment to the Father. Jesus was our example. He could have called legions of angels to set him free, but He chose to sacrifice himself for us, because He loves us. God knows the trials and tribulations of your heart, He knows sometimes you are hurting beyond what you feel you can handle. Sometimes we must do as King David did when there was no encouragement to be found anywhere. He encouraged himself in The Lord. Our Heavenly Father is right there to hold our hand, to hug us, and to lift our chin so we can concentrate on Him. As we press forward into our day, let us think of our spouse, our children. How can we, as servants of the Lord, children of the Most High, imitate Christ, and encourage ourselves in The Lord, then bring words of encouragement to them? Study your spouse, and your children. Then ask God to let the gift of encouragement be stirred up within so that you may be a blessing to someone else, instead of a lump under the sheets doing good for no one. Encourage yourself in The Lord, and then encourage another.

<u>Question for Dialogue:</u> How can I encourage you in those times when encouragement is most needed?

<u>Pray Together:</u> Lord, help us to lift up one another and never put each other down. Help us to be encouragers, not discouragers.

#9 Bigger Than Both of Us

"Don't be afraid of them. Remember The Lord, who is great and awesome, and fight for your brothers, your sons and your daughters, your wives and your homes" —Nehemiah 4:14b

Nehemiah spoke to his generation as they were rebuilding the walls of Jerusalem in the face of fierce opposition to encourage them, and to let them know that this was not just about their self-interests. This was about fighting for something greater than themselves. It was about their marriages, their families and their nation. As we look around to see the breakdown of the American family, it becomes clear that, once again, it's time to fight for our marriages our families and our nation. With the current attack on traditional marriage, and Christian standards of morality it's clear that we are in grave danger of passing on to our children a nation in moral chaos. This is no time to let our pettiness keep us from closing ranks against the outside enemies of marriage and family. It's time to quit whining selfishly, and fighting about meaningless issues. It's time to love one another as Christ loved us -unconditionally- and let that love impact a world searching for answers. It's time to let our children see the love of God in us. It's time to affect our communities for righteousness' sake. If we continue down the present path of immorality and chaos, our children will rise up to curse us for handing them a world in much worse shape than the world our parents handed us. Will our children rise up to bless us, or curse us? The answer will be determined by the choices we make today. Let's choose to give ourselves to a cause greater than self.

Question for Dialogue: Do you think we're doing all we can to impact our friends and family to reflect the Biblical values we profess?

Pray Together: Lord, help us to see that we have a responsibility to demonstrate to others what the love of God can do in a couple surrendered to Him.

#10 Communicate You Care

"The man runs away because he is a hired hand and cares nothing for the sheep. I am the good shepherd; I know my sheep and my sheep know me." —John 10:13

This week we heard from another couple that experienced a major breakthrough. Suddenly, strife was gone! They are actually talking to each other, and enjoying it for the first time in years! When I asked the wife about it she said, "He is so different. He's not angry all the time. He's talking and doing things in ways that show he's really trying." Then I asked the husband about it. He said, "I realize I have to do only one thing —communicate that I care." That's why Jesus said not only will the Good Shepherd lay down his very life for his sheep, but his sheep will know him. They will know he cares! That's why they listen to his voice. Are we caring as The Good Shepherd did, or are we more like the hired hand running off into our own little world of isolation while our marriages and families are lost to the wolves of this culture? It's simple, but not natural. It takes a conscious decision to choose to communicate you care. It's not enough to say you care if you don't communicate it effectively. If care isn't effectively communicated could it be that you really don't care enough for it to show? Ponder that one. You too, can have that breakthrough in your relationship. Put everything else on the back burner until you can effectively communicate you care. Be as the Good Shepherd, not the hired hand.

Question for Dialogue: How well do we communicate that we really care, especially in our attitudes and our tone of voice?

Pray Together: Lord, work in our hearts so that a genuine sense of care would be communicated in the way we speak to each other.

#11 A Team Sport

"Run in such a way as to get the prize"
—1 Corinthians 9:24b

We've been watching some of the Summer Olympics, and even there, we can't help but to see the lessons that can be learned to help us with our marriages.

During one event, I couldn't help but notice how one athlete tried to comfort and encourage a teammate when she fell off the pommel horse. There was no criticism, or disparaging remarks, but only comfort, assurance and encouragement. I thought, "That's the team spirit we need to see demonstrated in marriages if we are to win the prize in the Olympics of marriage and family relationships." How do you respond to your teammate –your spouse- when he or she "falls off the pommel horse" or makes a mistake? Are you there to encourage and lift up, or do you criticize and put down? Think about it. Would you like to have yourself for a teammate? If necessary, repent! Be a team that can bring home the gold. Run in such a way as to get the prize. You can do it –with God's help.

Question for Dialogue: Am I a good teammate? How can I encourage you when you make a mistake without putting you down for it?

Pray Together: Lord, help us to be better teammates to one another, so that we can run together in such a way as to win the prize.

#12 An Empty Nest

"...'My spirit will not leave them, and neither will these words I have given you. They will be on your lips and on the lips of your children..., I, the Lord, have spoken!'" — Isaiah 59:21

Well, the time has come. We're experiencing "The Empty Nest Syndrome," and if we haven't been working on our marriage that nest will feel totally empty when the children are gone. We all hurt in our own ways when a child goes off to college, or decides it's time to go on his or her own. We're facing this now. Our son has moved out, and our daughter will be getting married in a couple of months. My first thought, particularly as a Mom is "My babies; how will we make it without them?" Then we begin thinking of the trials they will face without us to help them. The reality is I miss my child! The hurt is felt in various ways, and tears are shed at unexpected times. That's normal. But if we don't remember who they really belong to, recovery will take significantly longer. Children are a blessing from God. They belong, not to us, but to Him. He blesses us by lending them to us for a season. We do the best we can loving, teaching, nurturing, training and enjoying them. Then, before we know it, it's time to release them into a world of chaos; that's difficult. Only our faith in God, and His promise to watch over them makes it manageable. The Bible promises that if we've taken the time to train them up in the way they should go, they won't depart from it. What that particular journey looks like is different for each one. Only God knows the way each should go. The one thing we can count on is God's promise to spread his wings over our children to keep them in the safety of His presence.

Question for Dialogue: Have we done all we can to prepare our children for life, and have we prepared ourselves for our empty nest?

Pray Together: Lord, help us to refocus in this new season in our lives; renew our love for you and for each other, and watch over our children as they pursue the plan you have for them.

#13 Expectations

"The wages of sin are death, but the gift of God is eternal life in Christ Jesus, our Lord."   –Romans 6:23

C.S. Lewis said that "there is nothing better than a Christian who knows himself, and no Christian who knows himself would dare think he deserves anything better than hell." C.S. Lewis was simply communicating the Gospel truth that if we received what we truly deserve we would all be burning in Hell. Because we are all sinners that's the only thing we have a legitimate right to; anything more is a bonus. How does that principle affect our relationships? If I expect dinner on the table at six o'clock sharp each night, when it's there I don't get too excited, because after all, it's expected. If it isn't there, look out! I get angry and everybody pays! Now if I don't expect it, and it's not there, I won't get upset; I didn't expect it. If it is on the table, wow! A bonus! I'll appreciate it because I didn't expect it. Apply the same principle to every part of your relationship, and you'll see that most of your anger and frustration comes because you're not getting something you expect, that you think you have a right to. Lower your expectations. If you expect nothing, then everything will be received as a gift. Your heart will reflect gratitude. That's where we want to be. Be careful not to insist on what you deserve. You might get it as C.S. Lewis reminds us. Be grateful. Be thankful, and begin working together from that place of mutual appreciation. If you woke up this morning to discover you were not burning in Hell, then you're already ahead of the game. Everything else is a bonus. So make no expectations or demands, but receive one another as a gift of God's grace.

Question for Dialogue: What expectations do we have of one another that continually causes dissatisfaction?

Pray Together: Lord, help us to realize that the only thing we really deserve is hell, and everything beyond that is because of your grace.

#14 Eyes on the Donut

"Finally, brothers, whatever is true, whatever is noble,... if anything is excellent or praiseworthy- think about such things." —Philippians 4:8

The apostle Paul gives us the secret to maintaining a positive attitude toward our marriage in this passage. You see, there are positives and negatives in every marriage. We all have certain blessings, gifts and things that God has done, and we all have problems, or things that God hasn't done for us. That's not the issue. The issue is, where we spend our mental time. Do we dwell on the things that God has done for us, or on the things that God hasn't done for us? That's the difference between having joy and peace, or being miserable the rest of your life. What is your mental address? I'm not saying we shouldn't acknowledge the negatives. That's just as dangerous. We need to bring them into the light and deal with them appropriately. But don't live in the negatives. Find whatever is good, whatever is right, whatever is praiseworthy, and magnify that, and guess what— you'll have more! The bottom line is that whatever you're dwelling on will reproduce itself in reality, whether it's positive or negative. So you may as well work on reproducing the positives. As someone once said,

"As you travels through life's journey, no matter what the goal, keep your eye on the donut, and not on the hole."

The donut represents the substance of what we have. The hole represents what we don't have. Keep your eye on the donut, not on the hole!

Question for Dialogue: Do we tend to dwell on the donut, or the hole?

Pray Together: Lord, help us to dwell on the blessings you've given us. We want more donut—less hole!

#15 Feelings

"Be completely humble and gentle; be patient, bearing with one another in love." —Ephesians 4:2

Relationships are about feelings, not facts. Sometimes a couple will come into our office, and one will begin to share feelings, and I'll look over to the other spouse to see a tipping back of the head and a rolling of the eyes that says, "Here we go again; of course I care. If I didn't care I wouldn't be here in the first place." or "Come on, you shouldn't feel that way. Of course I care." The issue isn't whether you care; it's whether or not your spouse "feels" cared for. It's all about feelings. Throw the facts out the window. When it comes to relationships we need to zero in on feelings, not facts or circumstances, or even truth (as we see it). This is usually more difficult for men since men think first, feel second. Women tend to feel first, and think second. Ask your typical male how he feels about something, and he'll look back at you with a blank stare that says, "What are you talking about?" The key is to ask him what he "thinks" about something first, then you can ask him how he feels about it. Now he'll have a thought to hang his feelings on. Ask a woman how she feels first, and then she'll be able to share what she thinks about it.

Doing all the right things won't meet the needs of the relationship if one spouse doesn't feel loved, and cared for by the attitude of the heart displayed in the tone of voice and body language of the other spouse. It's all about feelings.

Question for Dialogue: What things do we do or say that cause us to feel unloved or uncared for?

Pray Together: Lord, help us to be aware of the "feelings" that are caused by our communication, especially in our body language and our tone of voice. Help us to feel good about our relationship.

#16 Fig Leaves Don't Cover

"When the woman saw that the fruit of the tree was good… She also gave some to her husband, and he ate it. Then the eyes of both of them were opened, and they realized they were naked; so they sewed fig leaves together and made coverings for themselves." —Genesis 3:6, 7

This was the first "cover up." Adam and Eve felt guilt and shame, so they tried to cover up, but it didn't work. Then they tried to hide from God. That didn't work either. Unfortunately, not much has changed since then. We still try to cover up our sin and misdeeds with fig leaves of one kind or another. Maybe we'll try to compensate for our sin with other good deeds. Often single parents give children everything they want to try to make up for the failure of the marriage. I knew of a man who was having an affair. Each time he saw his mistress he brought home flowers to his wife to cover his own guilt. What a fig leaf! Others use alcohol or drugs to cover the shame. Anger makes for a good fig leaf. You know, "I'll get angry with you first so you won't dare challenge me on my sin." We've even learned how to use more noble fig leaves like pouring ourselves into our work. It doesn't matter; a fig leaf is a fig leaf. It will never cover, and so you continue to try to hide from God. What's the answer then? "The Lord God made garments of skin for Adam and his wife and he clothed them." (Genesis 3:21). And so it is with us. We must first "walk in the light" (be honest with God and with one another), surrender to Christ, and His blood will cleanse us of all sin. It doesn't just cover; it washes it away. Without the shedding of blood there can be no forgiveness. That's why fig leaves don't work, no matter how noble. Let's chuck the fig leaves; let's put on Christ!

Question for Dialogue: What are some of the "fig leaves" we have used to cover up some of our shortcomings?

Pray Together: Lord, help us to quit covering up, and to confess our shortcomings openly and honestly, so that the blood of Jesus can truly wash away our sin and we can continue to grow together.

#17 Fix the Problem

> *"By wisdom a house is built, and through understanding it is established; through knowledge its rooms are filled with rare and beautiful treasures."* —Proverbs 24:3,4

If I call a repairman to fix our dishwasher, and if he doesn't have the skill to fix my particular machine, but instead takes it upon himself to go about fixing the toaster, a lamp, and an electrical outlet, and then presents me with a bill for three hours of work, (while the dishwasher is still broke), should I pay him? Couldn't he argue that he did so much work, and after all, he did fix things that needed fixing. He may feel like he did a lot of work, and in fact, he did, but he didn't fix what was broke. Therefore no money! Well, it's no different with marriage. When there's a problem, no amount of work in other areas will bring us the reward we seek until we fix the problem. A husband could buy all the gifts in the world for his wife, but if she needs time with him, he's just wasting his money building a false sense of security thinking that he will compensate for what he hasn't fixed. Forget it. It won't work. Likewise, a wife who isn't sexually available for her husband shouldn't be lulled into thinking that a clean house will make up for a lack of sex. It won't happen. Don't get me wrong. Those other things are good. We should be buying gifts and keeping a clean house, but don't for a minute think they will compensate for what is broke in the marriage. You're simply wasting your energy. You might feel like you're working on your marriage, like the ill-trained repairman who certainly felt he was putting in a good day's work, but it's only wasted energy if you're not fixing what's broke. Identify the problem and fix what's broke.

<u>Question for Dialogue</u>: What are some of the things that are broke in our marriage that we have addressed by trying to fix something else?

<u>Pray Together</u>: Lord, help us to see what is really broke in our marriage and give us the wisdom and power to address the issue.

#18 Forgiveness and Forgivingness

> *"Bear with each other and forgive whatever grievances you may have against one another. Forgive as the Lord has forgiven you."* —Colossians 3:13

Forgiveness is a dynamic thing that must always be moving to be effective. The source of forgiveness is God. From him we receive forgiveness for our many sins, past, present and future. As we receive forgiveness the flow of grace cleanses us and makes us clean. Then, however, the flow must continue as we are forgiving others. If I stop the flow of grace by refusing to forgive my spouse, or anyone else, the river stops. The flow is halted. The water backs up and begins to grow murky as bacteria and germs begin to grow in the still, motionless water. In the same way, bitterness and anger begin to grow in my spirit if I stop the flow of grace. It becomes a bitter pool. I must let the living waters of grace flow by forgiving others even as I have been forgiven. The problem is that we often don't want to see others "get away with it" or "get off too easy." Don't worry about it. Forgiving others doesn't get them forgiven. Each one must present themselves, personally, to the throne of grace. Personal repentance is the only way one can receive true forgiveness. The only thing forgiving others really does is to release them to God for judgment instead of carrying the judgment in your own spirit. It also restores relationship. So, it's really for your own benefit to keep the flow moving by forgiving even as you have been forgiven. God cannot pour more forgiveness into a bitter pool backing up with unforgiveness and resentment. He can only pour it into a clear flowing stream. That's why Jesus taught that you cannot be forgiven unless you are forgiving.

Question for Dialogue: How is the flow of grace doing in our marriage? Is the river flowing? Where might it be stopped up?

Pray Together: Lord, help use to live in a state of forgiveness and forgivingness, so that your river of grace might flow freely.

#19 Fruit Inspectors

"But the fruit of the Spirit is love, joy, peace, patience, kindness, goodness, faithfulness, gentleness and self-control. Against such things there is no law." — Galatians 5:22, 23

My heart breaks each time I meet a believer who has known the Lord for a significant amount of time, and is still struggling with the same issues they struggled with before he or she same to know Christ. What happened in those years? Has there been no growth? Being born again is just the beginning. A newborn baby doesn't stay newborn. He grows. Yet, I'm sorry to say that many who are newly born into the Kingdom of God remain newborns. They simply don't grow. How can we tell how much we're growing? Don't go by how well one knows the Bible, or how active one is in church. That's no measure of Christian maturity. That only measures one's religiosity. Spiritual growth can only be measured by the fruit of God's Spirit evident in one's life. That's the true test. Take a look at each of the listed fruit and rate yourself on a scale of 1 to 10, (1 being the least, 10 meaning you've arrived.) How much of each of the Spirit's fruit is evident in your life? Then do the same for your spouse. Then sit down together and switch papers and dialogue on the subject. Then do it again next year, and the next, and the next, until Jesus comes for the harvest.

Question for Dialogue: What fruit of the Spirit is God trying to develop in each one of us? How?

Pray Together: Lord help us to remain under the hand of the Master Vinedresser as you help us grow and produce even more of the fruit of Your Spirit.

#20 Giving Freely

"Each man should give what he has decided in his heart to give, not reluctantly or under compulsion, for God loves a cheerful giver." —2 Corinthians 9:7

John was upset because his wife, Mary, wouldn't give him more sex. After expressing his anger every way he could, John convinced Mary that she wasn't being a "good Christian wife," so Mary began to give him more sex, but it just didn't satisfy. Why? Because Mary was doing it out of obedience, compulsion, a sense of obligation. Now John resented the fact that she "just wasn't into it." The truth is that John had her body, but he didn't have her heart. Every man wants to be desired. If there is no desire, sex becomes a ritual, through which both parties come to resent each other. What then is the answer to this timeless problem? John has to change his focus from the physical to the emotional. He has to set out to win Mary's heart again, and do whatever it will take to help her feel loved and cared for. The natural response will be a desire for relationship, which finds expression in a true heart-felt desire for sex. Then "love making" will be body, soul and spirit. She will want to make love more, because God will put it in her heart to give, and it will be genuine. John may continue to demand the physical act only to continue in his frustration and feelings of inadequacy, because he's not desirable, or he can work to meet Mary's emotional needs, and wait until God puts it in her heart to give, freely and unconditionally, simply because she loves and desires him. It may involve a waiting period, but it's more than worth the wait to receive not just sex, but love in all its fullness.

Question for Dialogue: Do we have sex, or do anything else because God has placed it in our hearts to do it, or do we give out of compulsion of obligation?

Pray Together: Lord, help us to forego giving out of a sense of compulsion, but put it in our own hearts to give freely and unconditionally. Help us win each other's heart.

#21 God Is in Control

> *"Then I heard what sounded like a great multitude, like the roar of rushing waters and like loud peals of thunder, shouting: "Hallelujah! For our Lord God Almighty reigns."*
> —Revelation 19:6

The older Penny and I get, the more we realize that we live our lives, not according to some deep philosophy, but rather by simple one-liners, like "God is in control." I remember when we were going through our most difficult times, how Penny would simply take a deep breath and declare, "God is in control." With that declaration we could then go on. You see, there's a sense of comfort in knowing that God is in control, and He won't let anything happen that isn't in our best interest, even when we can't see it. He is the God of the unknown, and because I know the God of the unknown is a good God, I can rest. I can let go. I may not understand everything that's happening. I may not even like it. But I can rest in knowing that God will work all things together for my good, if I will love Him, and remain available for His purposes (Romans 8:28). When I feel like things are getting out of control I don't have to grasp for control and add to the confusion. I can let go, because I know my God, who never sleeps, is on the job. I remember one individual who made up little signs and posted them all over her house to remind her that "God is in control." That just might be a good idea to remind us that The Lord Almighty reigns -and we need not worry, because "God is In control.

Question for Dialogue: When do we tend to panic and grasp for control? How can we remind each other that God is in control, so we don't have to be?

Pray Together: Lord, help us to abide in you and to be reassured that you are working all things together for our good because we live to please you.

#22 Growing in Oneness

"For he himself is our peace, who has made the two one and has destroyed the barrier, the dividing wall of hostility. Speaking the truth in love, we will in all things grow up into him, who is the head." -Ephesians 4:15

Although, Paul was speaking specifically about the dividing wall between Jews and Gentiles, the principle remains true for all relationships where dividing walls have been erected, even the dividing wall between a husband and a wife. We need to be honest with ourselves. Have we really surrendered our own self-wills to the will of God in our marriage? Have we really traded in our self-interests for His purposes? That's the only way the oneness can be achieved. Oneness is not the absorption of one personality into another. Oneness is found when both are willing to conform to God's will, so that it's no longer "my way" or "your way," but it's "His way." Our struggle is not to convince our spouse to our way of thinking. It's for both spouses to work together to find God's way of thinking in a given matter. Paul tells us how to do this. *"...speaking the truth in love, we will in all things grow up into him..."* To find that oneness centered in Christ we must be free to speak the truth in love without fear of rejection or judgment, and without trying to dominate our partner's will and thought patterns. No matter how uncomfortable, we must be able to share how we truly feel about the matter and have mutual respect for one another's feelings, whether we agree and understand it, or not. Our struggle is to work to find agreement concerning God's will, not our own. As we both remain submitted to the process we grow in oneness day by day. No one's identity gets lost, and God remains in the very center of our relationship.

Question for Dialogue: Have we been growing in oneness with God at the center of our relationship?

Pray Together: Lord, help us to put our self-wills aside, that we might be that threefold cord with you in the center.

#23 HEAD OF THE HOUSE?

> *"For he 'has put everything under his feet...When he has done this, then the Son himself, will be made subject to him who put everything under him, so that God may be all in all."*
> —1 Corinthians 15:27, 28

What does it mean to be the head of the house? Simply put, it means to be the head servant. God demonstrated his authority as the head of Christ by first putting everything under His feet. Then Christ made himself subject to the Father. That's the sequence. That's the way it happens. First, the husband places everything under the feet of his wife; then she willingly places herself under his authority, because it's safe. I've said it before -I don't know of a single woman who wouldn't gladly place herself under the authority of a man who would *first* lay the world at her feet. The key word is "first". Now please, I don't mean to give the wife whatever she wants. I certainly don't mean the husband is to be a doormat for the wife. I do mean the husband is to study and know her physical and emotional needs, and he must work to meet those needs. The husband is the initiator; the wife is the responder. As the husband first learns to serve his wife, unconditionally, she then begins to feel safe, and begins to place herself under his trustworthy and safe care. It must be a place of security and safety otherwise it won't work. If you have to demand it, then you surely don't have it. Learn to serve, unconditionally, and it will happen out of relationship, rather than compulsion, by grace rather than by law. That's biblical headship and submission.

Question for Dialogue: Is submission in our marriage out of compulsion or relationship? Are we both mutually submitted to Christ and to each other? Is servant leadership demonstrated in our home?

Pray Together: Dear Lord, help us to be better servant leaders, to live a life of service to one another out of reverence for you.

#24 Honor One Another

"Love must be sincere. Hate what is evil; cling to what is good. Be devoted to one another in brotherly love. Honor one another above yourselves." —Romans 12:9,10

Honor. That's not a word we hear too often in modern culture. Yet it is the very foundation of a lasting relationship. Without honor there can be no mutual respect. Without mutual respect there can be no intimacy. Without intimacy there is no real relationship. What does it mean to honor one another? It means to acknowledge ones' presence with a sense of awe. How would you respond if the most highly respected person you could think of walked into the room you were in? How would you respond to Jesus if he walked into the room? You would probably stand up as your mouth dropped open in awe. Wow! It's really Him! Hold on to that picture. That's the way we should respond to our spouse as they enter the room. "But he, or she isn't Jesus," you say. Maybe not, but isn't he or she the most important person in the world to you? If that's true, shouldn't there be a sense of awe in their presence? If that's not true, then I think you have some adjustments to make. When we feel honored we feel uplifted. That's what it means to honor one another "above yourselves." When we feel uplifted our basic need for significance and security is met freeing us to respond in a way that allows us to give respect and honor back, because we have first received it. Now both parties are lifting each other up instead of dishonoring one another, and tearing one another down. Treat one another, in the moment-by-moment events of the day like they are the most important person in the world to you. They are! Then remember, "Whatever you did for one of the least of these…you did for me" —Jesus.

Question for Dialogue: Do we really go out of our way to honor one another or do we dishonor one another in the way we speak?

Pray Together: Lord, help us to see one another as the most important person in the world, and let that feeling show up in the way we speak to each other—a sense of awe!

#25 Intimacy or Sex?

> *"The husband should fulfill his marital duty to his wife, and likewise the wife to her husband."* —1 Corinthians 7:1-6

Unfortunately, when I've heard this passage quoted it was usually a husband trying to convince his wife that her body belonged to him, and she had a Christian duty to give him sex whenever he wanted. Talk about twisting Scripture! All one has to do is look closely at this passage to see that Paul was talking about mutual respect, mutual desire and agreement. That's when sex becomes intimacy. Animals have sex; only God's human creation has the capacity for intimacy, a divine oneness in the sexual experience that grows out of mutual respect and mutual desire. Yes, it's a lot easier to settle for just sex, but ultimately it leaves one unfulfilled. The wife who is just doing her "wifely duties" by "servicing" her husband whenever he wants it will begin to resent him for making her feel used. She eventually loses respect for him and herself. The walls go up; intimacy is lost. True intimacy happens when we find that mutual respect, desire and agreement. Only then is there a chance to become one, not just physically, but emotionally and spiritually as well. You see, sex is a gift given to us by God to give us a taste of heaven here on earth. Just as we, who know Christ, will be one with Him one day, God allows us to experience a taste of that oneness here on earth. It's as close to heaven as we'll get this side of glory. Let's strive together to come to that mutual respect, desire and agreement. Then sex will be beyond all we can ask or imagine.

Question for Dialogue: Do we really enjoy our sexual experience because there's a sense of mutual desire, respect and agreement, or do we just go through the motions reluctantly?

Pray Together: Lord, help us build a sense of mutual respect and desire so that our sexual intimacy will be mutually fulfilling, and you'll get the glory!

#26 In the Moment

"Do not merely listen to the word, and so deceive yourselves. Do what it says." —James 1:22

Quite often we hear in the counseling room, "I love my wife, (or my husband), but he (or she) gets me so angry that I can't control myself in the moment." Bingo! That's where the problem is; it's *in the moment*. If we are not loving "*in the moment*" then we are not loving at all. One cannot say "I love you" while at the same time acting with anger. The two are mutually exclusive. That's like saying I'm a great Mets fan but I never watch a game or follow their scores, or saying "I have a million dollars for you in my bank account," but never withdrawing a penny for you. Actions are not consistent with the words, "*in the moment*," and that's where it counts. Love is not conditioned on the actions of the other person; it is unconditional; it is "*in the moment*". Even Jesus told us "What good is it to love those who love you, for even the Pagan do that..." (Luke 6:32). What He is saying is that godly love, loves "*in the moment*" regardless of ones circumstances. Yes, I know it's not natural. It requires the Holy Spirit, because it is the love of God, His love expressed through His disciple; that's you—*in the moment*!

Question for Dialogue: Do my actions in the moment communicate my love for you? Can you explain?

Pray Together: Lord, help us to communicate in truth and grace and love in the moment.

#27 Hula Hoop Therapy

"Wash away all my iniquity and cleanse me from my sin. For I know my transgressions, and my sin is always before me. Against you, you only, have I sinned and done what is evil in your sight..." —Psalm 51:2-4a

Imagine holding a hula hoop around yourself at waist level. Then repeat these words: "Everything inside this hula hoop I am responsible for and I can change with God's help, (My actions and my thoughts). Everything outside this hula hoop I am not responsible for and I cannot change, (Your actions and your thoughts)."

The husband is fully responsible for everything inside his hula hoop. The wife is fully responsible for everything inside her hula hoop. We need to take ownership for everything inside our respective hula hoops. Furthermore we need to keep out of each other's hula hoop. Wife, you can't change hubby. Quit trying. Get out of his hula hoop. Husband, you can't change wife; quit trying. Get out of her hula hoop. Worry about changing yourself, and by your example others will be influenced to positive change. That's leadership.

Question for Dialogue: Do we take responsibility for what's in our hula hoop? Do we stay out of each other's hula hoop?

Pray Together: Lord, help us to take full responsibility for everything inside our own hula hoops, and keep out of each other's hoop.

#28 Letter or Spirit?

"He has made us competent as ministers of a new covenant— not of the letter but of the Spirit; for the letter kills, but the Spirit gives life." —2 Corinthians 3:6

John and Mary decided to reconcile after they were both in adulterous relationships. They knew what the Bible said about marriage and they wanted to do the right thing. The problem was that instead of working toward redemption, they started putting so many conditions on each other that they spent all their time and energy playing the role of Sheriff waiting to catch each other in a "parole violation." Of course they were both hurt and were simply trying to protect themselves from further hurt, but the result was that they could never enjoy the redemptive grace of God because they were too busy accusing each other of their "parole violations." The reconciliation did not succeed. For reconciliation to be successful we have to put away our Sheriff badge and be continually forgiving even while we're being hurt. I know that sounds impossible; it is. That's why it takes the love of God. It is the love of God that "covers a multitude of sins." We can't go by the letter of the law; it will always kill. It's the Spirit of grace that gives life, liberty and restoration. It must be redemption, not probation.

Question for Dialogue: Do you feel like I've got you on probation and just waiting for you to commit a "parole violation?"

Pray Together: Lord help us to put away our Sheriff badges, and to love unconditionally trusting that you alone can judge rightly – and you will!

#29 It's All His Anyway

"The earth is the Lord's, and everything in it, the world, and all who live in it;" —Psalm 24:1

I often think about that day when I will stand before God, and hear Him say, "Well Bill, how did you do with that ministry I entrusted to you? How did you do with the house, car and all the other things I let you manage and use? Oh, and let's not forget the most important things I entrusted to you: How did you do with the marriage and family I let you manage?" Believe me, this will be no time for excuses. The Master trusted me to care for these people and things for Him. I will have to answer to Him. I guess it's only natural that I tend to care for things that don't belong to me better than I care for my own things. If I borrow something from a neighbor —say a lawn mower— I'm much more careful because I know it doesn't belong to me. If I break it, not only will the lawn mower have to be replaced, but I will have lost my friend's trust as well. He thought enough of me to trust me with his lawn mower. The least I could do is live up to that trust. If I would do that for a friend who lends me a lawn mower, how much more should I be responsible to care for those things and people entrusted to me by the God of the universe! We will all have to give account. Let's be sure we have no reason to be concerned.

Question for Dialogue: Do we really live like it all belongs to God, and He's concerned about the way we manage what He entrusted to us?

Pray Together: Lord, help us to be faithful stewards of all that you have entrusted to us so that we will have reason to hang our heads in shame when we see you.

#30 Follow Your Heart?—Not!

"The heart is deceitful above all things and beyond cure. Who can understand it?" —Jeremiah 17:9

One of the biggest lies deceiving an entire generation is one we still hear too often in the counseling room, "I have to follow my heart." It sounds so nice and pure, doesn't it? The truth is that divorce courts are filled with people who are following their hearts, and living to regret it after homes are broken and lives are ruined because someone just had to follow their heart. That's a formula for disaster. Why would anyone follow the heart when the heart is dumb! If the heart had any sense it would be a brain! God gave us brains to rule over our hearts. Yes, we must consider our hearts, and deal honestly with real feelings, but we must never be ruled by our hearts. We must consider the feelings of our hearts and process them through the mind God gave us. Then we can make intelligent decisions that will please God. Happiness is the result of obeying God with a willing heart. That's not often easy, but that must nevertheless be the goal of our spiritual growth. So it should be in marriage. Our hearts will deceive us. Let's use the mind God gave us to rule over our hearts, even when our hearts object. Let's press into God and His word until obedience to God will bring joy to our hearts, and our marriage and our lives will be a success.

Question for Dialogue: Do we tend to give into our feelings—following our hearts—or do we process them through the mind God gave us to make intelligent decisions?

Pray Together: Lord, increase our faith, and our self-control so that we can make decisions with the mind you gave us, and not give in to the deceitfulness of our own hearts.

#31 Listen to Understand

"By wisdom a house is built, and through understanding it is established" —Proverbs 24:3

Why do you listen? Do you listen to correct? To contradict? To defend yourself? To set them straight? If you can stop for a moment to examine your motive for listening, you can make some changes in your communication that will change the very nature of your marriage. We need to listen to one another for one reason, and one reason only—*to understand!* Effective communication begins with a desire to understand. Intimacy grows with understanding how we see and feel about things. Intimacy is "into-me-see." You can't do that by correcting or criticizing your spouse, or defending yourself. It's that simple! You may be right on the facts. In fact, you can be right all the way to divorce court, but that won't help the relationship. You must listen to understand. I didn't say you will understand. In fact, very often you won't! But your motive for listening has to be a desire, a "want to," to understand. This is a condition of the heart more than anything else. But only then can oneness begin and intimacy grow. In fact, that becomes the great adventure of growing together— understanding one another. Let your relationship be built on wisdom, and established through understanding. Yes, it takes patience, self-control and spiritual maturity, but the prize is so worth it! It's called intimacy!

Question for Dialogue: Do we listen to each other to understand or just to criticize, pass judgment or give our own opinion.

Pray Together: Lord give us the maturity and the self-control to listen to gain understanding. Our job is to understand. And on that foundation this house –this marriage- will be firmly established.

#32 Marriage, A Sacred Trust

"Marriage should be honored by all, and the marriage bed kept pure, for God will judge the adulterer and all the sexually immoral." —Hebrews 13:4

Here, in these United States same-sex unions have become legal, and are even called "marriage." One might say, "What has this got to do with my marriage? I've got enough problems without worrying about what other people call marriage." Though I understand the sentiment, it is not one we can entertain as Christians. Marriage was entrusted to us by God. What we see going on in the nation concerning marriage should motivate us to double our efforts to get it right, first in our own marriage, then to take it to the streets to do what we can to impact our society, so that our children, and theirs, will not grow up in Sodom, but will grow up in the nation we have known as "one nation under God." It's bigger than us! When the Old Testament Prophet, Nehemiah supervised the rebuilding of the walls of Jerusalem, he encouraged the people, *"Don't be afraid of them. Remember the Lord who is great and awesome and fight for your brothers, your sons and your daughters, your wives and your homes."* (Nehemiah 4:14b) We can do no less. Let's begin at home, then let's do what we can as we pray and work to advance the Kingdom of God. He gave all he had for us. Let's be prepared to give all we can for Him. Let's get in the fight!

Question for Dialogue: What are we doing, or what can we do to be a witness for the sanctity of marriage and family?

Pray Together: Lord, help us to appreciate the sacred trust you have given us in marriage, first concerning our own marriage. Then help us make a difference in our community, and even in the nation.

#33 Redeem the Times!

"See then that you walk circumspectly, not as fools but as wise, redeeming the time, because the days are evil. Therefore do not be unwise, but understand what the will of the Lord is."
—Ephesians 5:15-17

It's been said that there are just three kinds of people in the world: Those that make things happen, those that watch things happen, and those that just say *"Wha' happened?"* With seasons just seeming to fly by it often feels like time is slipping away, and we never got to do what we planned. Well, it's not too late. Maybe you can't change what you missed yesterday, but you can certainly begin making changes today. You can redeem the time, but it will take proactive measures on your part. It won't happen by itself, and don't wait for someone else to make it happen. Get a sense of what God's will is for you, your marriage and your family and make it happen. Don't buy into the excuses. There will always be reasons to put something off. Be an overcomer. Go with the reason for making it happen, and make it happen. Don't be one of those who will look back on your life and say, *"Wha' happened?"* Redeem the time; you can do it!

Question for Dialogue: What did we plan on doing this year that hasn't happened yet?

Pray Together: Lord help us to know your will, and set out to make it happen as you empower us to do so.

#34 No Jesus, No Peace

"If you, even you had only known on this day what would bring you peace -but now it is hidden from your eyes."
—Luke 19:42

We have more technological advancements, more knowledge, more resources, more wealth, more of everything, and less of the thing that matters most –peace, real peace. Now, with computers we even have more time to run more places, and do more things. Jesus looked over Jerusalem, and the Bible tells us he wept over what he saw—people who were running every which way, because they couldn't see what would bring them real peace. He wept because he saw into their future. He knew they were setting themselves up for a life of defeat, because they didn't recognize that the Prince of Peace was among them. They were too busy. How sad! Has anything really changed? Human nature is as changeable as a leopard's spots. I believe Jesus is still weeping over us today, because we're too busy to recognize that He is among us. What really brings peace is nothing other than the Prince of Peace, himself. Perhaps you've seen the bumper sticker: "No Jesus –No Peace." If our marriages and relationships are not centered in Christ, there will be no peace, No Jesus–No peace. Get as busy as you like. Work as much as you can. You'll still find no peace outside of Christ. Think about it.

Question for Dialogue: Do we have the peace of Christ in our relationship, in our home? What role does Jesus really play in our marriage?

Pray Together: Dear Lord, please come and take that central place you deserve in our marriage, and in our home. Let your peace rule in our lives.

#35 Don't Isolate

"A man who isolates himself seeks his own desire; He rages against all wise judgment." —Proverbs 18:1 (ESV)

It's interesting to see how two people who traveled with Jesus could mess up really bad, and yet one of them is used to start the Church, while the other one hangs himself on a tree until his guts spill out -ugh! What was the difference?

I'm talking about Peter and Judas. They both betrayed Jesus. Judas gave information that led to his capture. When he realized what he had done he was sorry. Peter denied Him three times; he even cursed Jesus just to convince people he wasn't one of his followers. What a wimp! But Judas hung himself, while Peter preached on the Day of Pentecost and 3,000 souls were saved, and the Church was born. What made the difference to bring such different outcomes? Judas isolated himself, where the enemy could convince him of self-destructive lies, while Peter stayed with others to pursue Christ.

You see, isolation leads to no good end. When we isolate or "stonewall" to keep others out of our lives, we also remain trapped inside, where the enemy of our souls can have a field day in our minds. Things don't get better; they get worse. It's in the darkness of isolation that the root of bitterness grows. Don't stonewall. Walk in the light. Be courageous; be there with others. Pursue Christ!

Question for Dialogue: When do you feel I tend to isolate myself, or stonewall you just to shut you out for my own reasons? How does that make you feel?

Pray Together: Lord, help us to resist isolating, stonewalling and keeping things to ourselves. Help us to walk in the light and to trust in God's grace as we pursue Christ with all that is within us.

#36 What Really Matters

"For in Christ Jesus neither circumcision nor uncircumcision has any value. The only thing that counts is faith expressing itself through love." —Galatians 5:6

Paul found the religious folk getting lost in arguments about things that were totally meaningless to God, and to the real issues of life. Has anything really changed? We still fight about everything from when and where we should worship to who should throw out the garbage. I believe God is still saying what Paul was saying, *"Enough already! Quit arguing about meaningless junk."* What matters isn't the things of this world, but faith expressing itself through love. If you don't have faith expressed in love it doesn't matter who throws out the garbage, or when and where you worship. These meaningless arguments have to do with this temporal life, but faith expressing itself in love is the vehicle that begins in this life to carry us into eternity to be with Jesus and those we love who also know Him. That's what matters! Let's not get lost majoring in the minors. Let's not let the enemy of our marriages, and our souls, distract us from the mission to love with all our hearts, soul and strength. Whenever we sense the enemy trying to tempt us into a meaningless squabble simply ask yourself, "In light of eternity, is this really important?" I guarantee, if you will ask yourself that question regularly you will find an immediate drop in meaningless squabbling. In light of eternity, is it really important? What matters is faith expressing itself through love. Try it. It works!

Question for Dialogue: Do we get caught up in meaningless squabbles? Over what?

Pray Together: Lord, help us to focus on the things that matter to you. Keep us from getting caught up in meaningless squabbles. Help us to focus on your limitless love that it may flow between the two of us, so that the world will see Jesus in our marriage.

#37 Road Work

"For we are God's workmanship, created in Christ Jesus to do good works, which God prepared in advance for us to do."
— Ephesians 2:10

There is major construction going on right outside our front door. It's a noisy distraction, and I confess, I'm sometimes tempted to grumble under my own breath about the inconvenience, especially when I have to carefully navigate through the orange construction barrels and newly created potholes just to get into my driveway. I have to continually remind myself, "They are just doing their job to make this a better place to live and work. When it's completed I'll be glad for the improvements. In the meantime I just need to exercise patience and grace." Then I realized it's much the same way with marriage. Sometimes things get messy, and even noisy around the construction site God is working on –us! But it is God engineering the project to conform us into the image of Christ according to the plans He had drawn up long before we had a clue about anything. So, it may be inconvenient at times, and we may have to navigate carefully around potholes and construction barrels in our relationships, but let's do so with patience and grace while God is making some very necessary improvements in our marriage. It can only get better!

Question for Dialogue: Do you feel like our marriage is a construction site which requires careful driving avoiding barriers and potholes? Can you explain? How do you think the project will look differently when they next phase is completed?

Pray Together: Lord, help us to have patience and grace for one another, without grumbling or griping, as you are working to make improvements. Help us keep our eyes on the blessing the improvements will bring.

#38 YOU ARE AN EXAMPLE

"Follow my example, as I follow the example of Christ."
—1 Corinthians 11:1

Your children will be like you. They are catching whatever it is that you have, and following your example, for better or for worse. The real question is which way are you leading your children? Are you leading them up, or are you leading them down? I remember attending a fellow minister's 70th birthday party during which time each of his children, now grown with families of their own, stood up and spoke of their Dad. The one thing that impressed me, and brought some conviction to my own heart, was how each one said that what they remembered most was how every morning, when they awoke, they would always find their Dad in his den with his Bible on his knees in prayer. What an example! Though prayer has always been a regular part of my life, I was not quite that public with it, or as regular. Though I prayed continually, my children didn't see it most of the time. Now, I know I can't change the past, but I can ask God's forgiveness for my shortcomings as a Christian husband, and father, and purpose in my heart to set the example from this day forward to lead my family up, not down, so that they can fulfill their potential in Christ. His blessings are new every morning, and great is his faithfulness. We are an example; let's be the right example!

Question for Dialogue: What type of an example are we presenting to our children and family? Let's be honest.

Pray Together: Lord, help us to follow Christ in word and in deed, so that our children will have the example they will need to succeed.

#39 THE "S" WORD

"And be subject to one another in the fear of Christ."
—Ephesians 5:21 (NASB)

Some Bible translations use the "S" word. You know, "submit." Yuck! No one likes the word, much less the idea of submitting to a spouse. But, doesn't the Bible say wives are to "submit to your husband?" For many, there has already been an unconscious decision made, "I will never submit to you!" The problem is our misuse of the word. The Bible clearly presents a sense of mutual submission. It begins with the husband, as the leader, submitting to his wife, honoring and esteeming her more highly than himself. Then she naturally responds by returning the honor. She submits to him, and now they are being "subject to one another in the fear of Christ." You see, we submit to one another as an expression of our reverence for Christ. In other words, our submission to Christ is demonstrated in our submission to each another! Too many of us have lost the sense of "the fear of The Lord." We've forgotten how to revere Christ, to honor Him, and yes, even submit to Him. So we carry that same rebellion into our human relationships. We struggle with the "S" word. We need to be honest and open with God and confess, our rebellion, self-righteousness and stubbornness, and submit ourselves to Jesus first, then to our spouse, in the fear, extreme reverence, and holy awe of our God. Then our love for God will be seen in our love –our mutual submission- for one another.

Question for Dialogue: How well do we do in submitting to each other?

Pray Together: Help us to truly live a life "in the fear of Christ" with a holy awe and reverence that will be reflected in the way we treat and love one another.

#40 Loving Leadership

"Be completely humble and gentle; be patient, bearing with one another in love." —Ephesians 4:2

When it comes to the role and responsibility of husbands and fathers it seems like we have gone from one extreme to another in our culture. In a little more than a generation we've gone from dictator to abdicator. One is just as unbiblical, and as damaging to healthy families as the other. Somehow, we need to come back to this issue and find balance. The natural tendency is to surrender all responsibility when our authority is met with resistance, i.e., "You won't listen to me, so do it yourself!" But the end result is visionless chaos. As men of God, we must lead with the fierceness of the Lion of Judah, and yet with the tenderness of the Lamb of God. We must be, as one author put it, "Tender Warriors." We must be fully engaged without making demands, but rather by our example, inspiring others to follow. Wives can help by encouraging us when we get it right, and gently and respectfully helping us make course corrections when we don't. Husbands and fathers must step up to the plate and lead. If we're not sure how to do it, we need to look to the One who leads us, Jesus Christ. In fact, we can't effectively lead others unless we are under His leadership. Let's purpose in our hearts today to provide that which our families are crying out for –Loving Leadership!

Question for Dialogue: Is there balanced leadership in our home between tyrant leadership and abdicated leadership? How so?

Pray Together: Lord, help us to find the right balance, no longer to go from dictator to abdicator, but to provide loving pro-active leadership. Help us to encourage one another with tenderness and respect.

#41 The Power of Two

"Again, I tell you that if two of you on earth agree about anything you ask for, it will be done for you by my Father in heaven." —Matthew 18:19

In the very beginning, God said it's not good for man to be alone. Throughout the Bible we see a special power when two are united. Yet, if we had to describe the problems we see in our counseling office, in general, they all come down to feelings of "aloneness." Husbands and wives, though married, in some cases for many years, feel very much alone. There is no oneness, no "we"-ness. It's all about me. Instead of being a team, husbands and wives have adopted a mentality of radical individualism, so it's no wonder they feel alone. Alone, God gave Adam the mission to tend a garden. Together, with Eve he was commissioned to take dominion over all the earth. And so it is today. Alone, we can barely take care of ourselves. But two, working together in mutual agreement can do anything God has called them to do. We must purpose in our hearts to do nothing unless there is mutual agreement. Let your struggle be to find that mutual agreement before you move forward, and together, nothing will be impossible for you.

Question for Dialogue: Are we a team? Do we think "we," or is it more about "me"?

Pray Together: Lord help us to give up our self-centeredness so that we will work to find unity and oneness, so that together, we can take dominion over all the powers that come against our marriage and our family

#42 Whose Body Is It Anyway?

> *"The husband should fulfill his marital duty to his wife, and likewise the wife to her husband. The wife's body does not belong to her alone but also to her husband. In the same way, the husband's body does not belong to him alone but also to his wife."* —1 Corinthians 7:3, 4

I was recently challenged by an irate husband who said we were teaching feminist theology -whatever that is- because we teach that it's not enough for a wife to give herself sexually to her husband if she can't do it with a willing heart. He said, "Don't you know the Bible says the wife's body belongs to the husband. She should submit to her husband whenever he has a need." I said, "Amen, on the first part brother, but let's look at the second part of that verse: "...The husband's body does not belong to him alone but also to his wife." So then, each body equally belongs to the other. Though the husband may want his wife's body under him, she may want his body on the other side of the bed! Each one has equal authority, as verified by Ephesians 5:21: "Be submitted one to another out of reverence for Christ." So you see, it's not a matter of whose body belongs to who, for we all belong to God. (Psalm 24:1) The issue is about giving freely to each other out of a willing heart. Yes, it may be more of a challenge to win the heart than to demand the body. But that's love. Anything else is selfishness.

Question for Dialogue: Is our relationship one that comes from willing hearts, or do we simply try to manipulate one another to get our own needs met?

Pray Together: Lord help us to freely give to one another as you have freely given yourself for us. Let our relationship be built out of a love in our hearts, and not a need in our flesh.

#43 Marriage Training

"...train yourself to be godly. For physical training is of some value, but godliness has value for all things, holding promise for both the present life and the life to come."
— 1 Timothy 4:7, 8

Who would ever think of such a thing as marriage training? That's ridiculous! Is it really? Why are so many marriages failing? They simply haven't been trained. You see, training is more than learning. An athlete can know how to excel in his sport and have all the right information stored in his memory, but if he has not trained himself to apply the knowledge he will not succeed. Just as an athlete must assess his weaknesses and work to strengthen him in those areas until they are developed, so too, we must assess our marriages, identify the weaknesses and put ourselves on a program to build them up. It's not enough to read another book, or attend another seminar. We must go into training. First, find a coach who will hold you accountable, perhaps, a friend, a pastor or a counselor. Make sure it's someone who will love you enough to tell you the truth even when you don't want to hear it. Then assess the strengths and weaknesses of your marriage, and start doing whatever it takes to train yourself to develop your relationship muscles to build a strong marriage. It's a process, and it will be work. You know how the saying goes, "No pain, no gain." And so it is with marriage. So keep your eye on the prize—a marriage that will bring fulfillment and love to each of you, a model for your children, and ultimately, reflect the glory and the grace of God to a world without hope. That's the "gold." As difficult as the training may be, it's just so worth it!!

Question for Dialogue: What are some of the weak areas in our marriage that could use some "marriage training?"

Pray Together: Lord, help us to go into training in a purposeful way to develop those areas that need attention so that we will win the gold when it comes to our marriage.

#44 TIMES OF REFRESHING

> *"Repent, then, and turn to God, so that your sins may be wiped out, that the times of refreshing may come from The Lord, and that he may send the Christ who has been appointed for you -even Jesus."* —Acts 3:19

Since I was feeling a little worn out today I felt led to write about, "the times of refreshing." I needed refreshing for myself, so I turned to the third chapter of Acts where I remembered Peter spoke about the subject, and there it was, big as life: <u>*REPENT ... then turn to God...that the times of refreshing may come.*</u>

Who wants to hear that? But nevertheless, there's no way around it. In fact, that is the very key to experiencing the times of refreshing. We need to be able to stand before God, drop our fig leaves, and be open and honest with God and one another that the refreshing winds of the Holy Spirit can blow over us and into every part of our lives. We need to repent and be honest not just about our actions but also about our feelings and thoughts. Of course, we need to use wisdom on timing and substance concerning what and how we share, but we need to share, honestly. If our actions, thoughts or opinions are not pleasing to God, then we need to get on our knees and ask God to change our hearts; make us new. God is looking for that heart that is, first of all, honest, then desiring to change to be pleasing to Him. The only sin God cannot forgive is the one we don't confess to Him. So, let's quit justifying, rationalizing or minimizing our sin. Let's call it for what it is. Let's repent, and experience the times of refreshing that God so much wants us to experience.

Question for Dialogue: What are some of the areas in my life that need repentance and a fresh wind of the Holy Spirit to blow over them?

Pray Together: Lord, help us to gently share with one another where we think repentance is needed, and help us both to be refreshed by repentance as we grow together in Him.

#45 Relationships or Volley Balls

"Be devoted to one another in brotherly love. Honor one another above yourselves." –Romans 12:10

In the Tom Hanks movie, "Castaway," a business executive who lives for his work finds himself alone on a desert island with only a volleyball to talk to. I thought it interesting that there was absolutely no mention of God in a situation where one would reasonably expect even an agnostic to be found challenging God to prove he existed by coming to his aid. The story, however, serves to illustrate that what really is important in life is relationships. Relationships are precious. When unforeseen circumstances cause us to lose relationships, it's sad. When, by our own actions, we fail to provide the time and energy needed to maintain and build our relationships, that's foolishness. The real question is, "Will we have more than a volley ball to relate with?" Have we spent time building relationship with God, with one another? That takes time and focus, not talking about the job, or the children, or the house, but focus on one another's feelings and needs. The most punishing enemy of the human soul is loneliness. It's easy to be lonely in a crowded room. It's easy to live in a house filled with lonely people. It's also sad. Everyone's busy with their own lives, but are we building a life in common? What will you have down the road in a few years, meaningful relationships, or a volleyball to talk to? Is it time to make some changes?

Question for Dialogue: How are we doing building and maintaining our relationships with God, with each other and with friends?

Pray Together: Lord help us to focus on relationships so that we'll have more than a volley ball to talk to.

#46 REPENTANCE...UGH!

> *"From that time on Jesus began to preach, 'Repent, for the Kingdom of Heaven is near.'"* —Matthew 4:17

Repentance? That's not a word that brings warm fuzzies. Who needs it? Can't we just talk about God's love, and how we will all go to heaven if we just mean well? Sorry! Jesus' first message was not "God loves you." It was "Repent!" The truth is that we can't know God's love without first repenting, changing our ways, turning from what we think is right to what He says is right. Only then can we know His love for us. Our sin occupies space that His love seeks to displace. When a client asks me how they can hear God's voice my standard answer is "Ask Him to tell you what your sins are, and I'll bet you'll hear Him." You know what? It works every time. As God reveals your sin make a list, and begin choosing to change your mind, and pray for the power to change. God will provide the power, but He leaves the choice up to you. If you don't make the choice, He can't provide the power. I've seen lives change dramatically at the altar, but I've seen more lives change day by day, sin by sin, repentance by repentance. The good news is that every act of true repentance opens us to enjoy more of God's love. His love is always there, but our ability to receive it is hindered by our sin. Be bold and courageous. Choose to repent. Turn from your "wicked" ways. Turn to God's ways. Make a list of the sin that God reveals to you when you ask Him in prayer. Then choose to change one by one, little by little, and know more love as you go—as you grow. The alternative is nothing less than missing Heaven and knowing hell. There's no in-between. Sorry!

Question for Dialogue: How often do we really take inventory of our own sin? Do we talk about our own sin, or just point the finger at each other?

Pray Together: Lord, help us to take an honest inventory of our own sin, accountable to each other as we begin to change our ways sin by sin, that we might enjoy more and more of your love for us. Help us to repent for the Kingdom of Heaven is truly at hand.

#47 Respond vs. Reacting

"Set a guard over my mouth, O Lord; keep watch over the door of my lips." —Psalm 141:3

What kind of a prayer is that? Unfortunately, it's probably a prayer that most of us need to be praying more often. Too often we blurt out things that we wish we could take back. Sometimes, even as they are leaving our mouths we wish somehow they could make a u-turn and come back into our mouths before they go out and kill. Don't feel bad. It's natural. But just because it's natural that doesn't mean it's good. If you stand in front of me while I cross my legs and tap my knee with a small rubber mallet, you're going to get kicked by my very natural reflex. That's what we do to each other when we just blurt out what's natural. But wait a minute. Didn't God make us a little higher than the animals? Didn't he give us a brain so we could choose our responses instead of going with our natural reflex like any baboon? He sure did! That's why we can _choose to respond_ instead of reacting. But it will take using the brain God gave us. Next time you're tempted to react reflexively, stop, think, then let the words that come out of your mouth be a product of an intelligently thought out response instead of a baboon reflex. Respond instead of reacting.

Question for Dialogue: How do I let you push my buttons that causes me to react without thinking? How do I push yours?

Pray Together: Lord, help us to learn to respond instead of reacting so that our marriage will be a product of an intelligently thought out plan instead of a product of our natural base instincts.

#48 Your In-House Counselor

"And I will ask the Father, and He will give you another Counselor... that is the Spirit of truth, whom the world cannot receive..." —John 14:16

We have had clients who, on occasion, would say to us, "We wish we could take you home to be there when we have our knock-down drag-out fights." Apparently, they feel that if a counselor were available in the heat of battle they would find resolution to their communication problems. The truth is that God has provided exactly that for every couple. You have a live-in Counselor who is better than any human counselor. He is the ever-present Holy Spirit. The problem is that He isn't visible to the natural eye. He is residing inside each believer waiting to be called upon to bring justice and grace into every situation. But just as the one must agree to come to our office to listen to what we have to say, one must also agree to come to the place of acknowledging God's presence—the Holy Spirit—among them, and listen to what He has to say. How do they do that? By praying and searching the Scriptures together; by setting aside their self-interests and submitting to the interests and will of God concerning their situation as revealed through the Word and prayer. The Holy Spirit will reveal the will of God that always tends toward reconciliation to himself, then to one another. Paul tells us exactly where to find this Counselor: "Don't you know that you are God's temple and that God's Spirit lives in you?" (1 Cor. 3:16). Go ahead, make an appointment with Him. The best part? The fee was already paid on Calvary's cross.

Question for the both of us: When was the last time we both submitted ourselves to seeking counsel from the Holy Spirit together?

Prayer For Both of Us: Lord, help us to mutually submit to the counsel of your Holy Spirit. Help us to call upon Him, daily, together, that this marriage will become, "*a cord of three strands that is not quickly broken.*"

#49 THE LANGUAGE OF INTIMACY

"Many will say to me... 'Lord, Lord, did we not prophesy in your name,...drive out demons and perform many miracles?' Then I will tell them plainly, 'I never knew you. Away from me, you evildoers!'" --Matthew 7:22, 23

How could Jesus be so cruel to call his followers evildoers? After all, they were doing the work of the ministry, yet He said He never knew them. How could this be? The answer lies in the word He used when he said, "I never *knew* you." He was saying, "You and I were never intimate. You are doing your own thing in my Name, without taking the time to know me, intimately." You see, without intimacy you have ritual instead of relationship. What keeps marriages strong and healthy is not ritual, but a relationship that grows out of deep intimacy.

We build intimacy, (or "into-me-see"), by sharing feelings and needs. There are five levels of communication from the most superficial to the most intimate: speaking in clichés, sharing facts, sharing opinions, sharing feelings and sharing needs. Only the last two levels, sharing feelings and needs, actually build intimacy. That only happens when we take the time to sit down face-to-face, heart-to-heart, to really get to know, and understand one another.

<u>Question for Dialogue:</u> Can we safely share our true feelings and needs without fear of being judged, rejected, corrected or discounted?

<u>Pray Together:</u> Lord, help us to know each other by taking the time to share our feelings and our needs. Help us find true intimacy with you, and with one another.

#50 THE LIGHT IN YOU

"The eye is the lamp of the body. If your eyes are good your whole body will be full of light. But if your eyes are bad your whole body will be full of darkness. If then, the light that is within you is darkness, how great is that darkness!"
—Matthew. 6:22-24

Each of us has a light source. If it is truly light then that light energy will be projected through our eyes, the lamps of our bodies. Everything will be more brightly illuminated. The grass will be greener. They sky will be bluer, because the light that is in you is projected on everything around you. But if that light in you is darkness, then that darkness will be projected. It will be like a shadow cast upon everything you look at. The grass will be drab and the sky will be gray. If the light in you is light you will see the things that God has given you in your relationship with your spouse. You will be counting your blessings. If the light in you is darkness, that darkness will be projected onto all the things God hasn't given you in your marriage. You will see the negatives, and not the positives. The lesson for marriage in these verses is that, though there are positives and negatives in every marriage, whether we're walking in the light of his love and joy, or in darkness and misery, has more to do with the light source in us than our actual circumstances. In His light we see light. If things look bleak out there it's time to check the light source in here!

Question for Dialogue: Do you think the light in me is light or darkness? Explain.

Pray Together: Lord, help the light in us be truly the light of Christ so that we will see your goodness and blessings wherever we look.

#51 The Place of Peace

"You will keep in perfect peace all who trust in you, whose thoughts are fixed on you." —Isaiah 26:3

Throughout our day-to-day lives, we often run into circumstances that one of us wants to change, but the other one is just not that willing, at least, not right now. In our humanity we want things to work as we plan, or at the very least, meet our minimum expectations for the situation. When was the last time you had your mind set to go out and buy something, and your spouse just wasn't ready? Do you find yourself frustrated and tired of waiting on your mate? Some of us are of the mindset "I want it done yesterday," or "I want to do this now, my way." Have you ever tried to invite God into such a situation? Can you see yourself asking Him to take control instead of yourself? The next time you find yourself thinking like this, pull on the reigns of your mind. Tell yourself, out loud if you must, "WHOA!" Then command your mind to turn your thoughts over to the Lord. Release all expectations and just thank Him for the outcome. When I am able to do this, peace comes over me, and sometimes my spouse even sets aside his agenda to put me above his plans. When that happens it's really special because I know it's coming from his heart, not because he's just trying to keep me quiet. But it does take trust. It takes keeping my mind fixed on Him.

Question for Dialogue: Do you think I tend to lose my peace when I don't get my way?

Pray Together: Dear Lord, please help us to mutually agree to seek you in all things and to love each other in spite of unmet expectations. Keep us in your perfect peace as our minds stay fixed on you.

#52 THE POWER OF LIFE AND DEATH

"The tongue has the power of life and death, and those who love it will eat its fruit." —Proverbs 18:21

I always thought it interesting that in the Genesis account of creation we're told that God created the earth, not by fashioning a lump of clay, or mixing up some earthly concoction in his chemistry lab, but rather we're told that "God said..." and "there was..." What a powerful word! He simply said it, and it was! Jesus told his disciples that if they would "say" to this mountain be thou removed it would jump into the sea! Talk about power! I'd love to say, "bills be paid!" and see it happen. Oh well, I guess I'm still missing something.

But nevertheless, there is power in the spoken word to create or to destroy. I've seen too many people come into our counseling office living a life of defeat, never finding their potential, because of a parent who spoke defeat into their lives. The power of words! The tongue has the power of life and death. It is an instrument for creation or destruction. If you could visually see the words go out of your own mouth would you see them lifting up others or would it go toward putting them down? Would they build up or tear down? It's no wonder the Bible tells us we'll have to give account for every idol word that proceeds from our mouths. With our tongues we can create or destroy, bless or curse. Out of our mouths should pass nothing but truth, life and blessing. Let's create not destroy.

Question for Dialogue: What do I see coming out of your mouth, words that build up or words that tear down? What do you see coming out of my mouth?

Pray Together: Lord, help us to let nothing pass through our lips that will destroy what you are trying to create in our lives. Help us to speak nothing but truth, life and blessing. Help us to be part of your plan for creation.

#53 Truth and Grace

"From the fullness of his grace we have all received one blessing after another. For the law was given through Moses; grace and truth came through Jesus Christ." —1 John 1:17

Grace is the medium for truth. In an atmosphere of grace truth can flow unhindered. In truth there is freedom to love, to learn and to grow. Truth and grace are partners that keep us balanced, and Christ-centered. It's not uncommon for a husband to hide a decision he has made from his wife, because he was afraid of what her reaction might be. It's not uncommon for a Mom to keep things about the children from Dad, because she might be afraid he would be too hard on the children. No grace. In both cases there is no intent to lie, but the effect, in fact, is a lie. We are not walking in truth. In many cases husbands and wives are living lies, because there is no grace, and therefore no truth. A husband who is always angry, or a wife who is always nagging, make it impossible for truth to flow in an atmosphere of grace.

Jesus told us that we shall know the truth, and the truth will set us free. Before we can be freed by the truth we must establish the atmosphere in which truth can flow freely—the atmosphere of grace. God has shown us grace by not holding our many sins against us. Now it's up to us to extend that grace to others. If we have not received it personally, we don't have it to give. You'll only get frustrated. First you must choose to live for Christ, and receive His grace. Then you will have it to give to your spouse. Then truth can flow. Then you can grow together in His love in truth and grace.

Question for Dialogue: What is the atmosphere in our home? Is it grace, or is it strife and tension? How can we have more grace for one another, and therefore, more truth?

Pray Together: Lord, help us to receive the fullness of your grace that we would have it for one another.

#54 Marriage and Politics

> *"Then he said to them, 'Give to Caesar what is Caesar's, and to God what is God's.'"* —Matthew 22:21

At first, one might wonder what in the world politics would have to do with marriage? The truth is politics has everything to do with marriage. First of all, marriage is an institution ordained by God, as the sacred union between a man and a woman. One of its primary purposes is to represent the relationship God desires to have with His creation. We are betrothed to Him when we receive Christ as Savior. He, the bridegroom, will come for his bride to consummate the marriage at the last trumpet call. Therefore, marriage is a sacred institution created by, defined by, and overseen by God himself. This sacred institution is the very foundation for civil order. We, who are married, have the honor and privilege of representing this nature of God on the earth. Marriage is not about us. It's about God, His kingdom, and His order for a humanity.

Now it is the duty of civil authorities to help facilitate this divinely given institution without usurping God's authority by redefining it according to human whims.

We must fulfill our responsibility to our nation as part of our responsibility to God, to vote for godly men and women who will submit to the divine authority of God and His definition of marriage—no other. Jesus instructed us to give unto God what is God's, and unto Caesar what is Caesar's, namely, our informed vote. Marriage and the rest of societal order hang in the balance. The charge to us: ***Pray and Vote!***

Question for Dialogue: Do we take our responsibility to vote seriously enough to vote on every Election Day.

Pray Together: Lord, help us to be faithful in our stewardship of liberty and vote to protect the holy institution of marriage.

#55 Two Are Better

> *"Two are better than one because they have a good return for their work: If one falls down his friend can help him up.... but a cord of three strands is not quickly broken"*
> —*Ecclesiastes 4:9-12* (NLT)

The preacher here teaches about the benefits of working together, walking together, even sleeping together. Unless one has the gift of celibacy they are not really complete until there is unity with a spouse. Scripture tells us that the effectiveness of two is not just doubled—*it's multiplied*! Deuteronomy 32:30 says though one man can chase a thousand two can put ten thousand to flight! No wonder the enemy of our souls has been so intent on destroying marriages. A solid married couple is the biggest threat to Satan's plans to destroy our families and culture. Many of the ills we see in our society can be traced back to broken families. As the marriage goes, so goes the family, so goes the church, so goes the society. But a couple wrapped around Jesus—the picture of the cord of three strands—that is not easily broken. Nothing will be impossible for a husband and wife dedicated to keeping Christ in the center of their relationship, and wrapped tight around Him and one another. When we sense the spirit of strife approaching, that's when we have to close ranks against Satan. Forget about what we want, and ask, "What is it that Jesus wants?" Two is a gift from God. A threefold cord is unbeatable!

Question for Dialogue: How have we been there for one another in times of need? Have we kept Christ in the center of our relationship?

Pray Together: "Lord, help us keep you in the center of our marriage, and day-to-day lives, wrapped around you tightly.

#56 When We're Apart

"I belong to my lover, and his desire is for me."
—Song of Solomon 7:10

In this day and age our commitments to our families and jobs leave us little time to just enjoy one another, especially starving for time is the most important of human relationships—husband and wife.

Bill and I have spent one of our very few weekends apart this weekend, and at first I saw it as an opportunity to get needed things done. I knew I would miss him, but I also knew I could accomplish so much with him away. I could actually have a time alone! Funny, instead of hearing God say, "Come away with me," I sensed Him saying, "Can you really feel the absence of your other half?" Not what I expected Lord!

As I lay my head down on the pillow 2:30 A.M Sunday morning my best friend wasn't with me. His caring arms weren't around me. Did I miss him? YOU BET I DID! Yet God was there and spoke of His love for me. So I rested! I awoke this morning knowing that God has done a great thing in my very own heart. I know that God has given me a special blessing in the spouse He provided—and even more than that—I know "I belong to my beloved and his desire is for me." I am awaiting Bill's return with an excited anticipation of renewing our love affair all over again. I want to, once again, receive the gift God has so graciously given to me.

<u>**Question for Dialogue**</u>*:* How do I feel when we're apart? Have we learned to appreciate each other sufficiently so that when we are apart we feel a sense of loss?

<u>**Pray Together:**</u> Lord, help us to take time daily to connect so that we can build an intimacy that will result in a sense of loss and appreciation for one another when we are apart.

#57 WHO OR WHAT?

"The LORD God said, "It is not good for the man to be alone. I will make a helper suitable for him." —Genesis 2:18

If God gave you a gift, beautifully wrapped with a note on it which said "Do Not Open Until Christmas," what would you do with it? Would you take it home and care for it? For all you know it could be just a lump of coal in the box. "But that's not important," you say. What's important is that this gift was given by God! Whatever is in the box is special just because of the One who gave it. That's why you'll value it, and guard it with your life. Now what will happen when Christmas comes and you open it to find, yep, you got it —a piece of coal. If you look at it simply for what it is there would be no reason to care for it, but if you'll see it for who gave it to you, it will be your most prized possession. So it is in marriage. If we look at each other for what we are, we will all fall short. We see the faults in one another. It's like we brought home a beautifully wrapped gift from Church when we said "I do." Then when we got home we started unwrapping it to discover a hunk of coal. Now what do we do with it? Do we build disdain for it because it isn't what we thought it was, or will we value it for who gave it to us—*God himself*! What my spouse is will always fall short of my standard, just as I will fall short of hers. I can't love her for what she is. Thank God He didn't love me for what I am. I'm a self-centered sinner. But He loved me for who I am—his very own creation. In the same way, I want to love my spouse for who she is—God's gift to complete me where I am incomplete, a helper suitable for me, given to me by the very hand of God. A diamond in the making. Wow!

Question for Dialogue: Do I see you for who you are, or for what you are? How do you see me?

Pray Together: Lord, help us to see each other for who we are, your gift to each other to complete us where we are incomplete.

#58 Who to Please

"Am I now trying to win the approval of men, or of God? Or am I trying to please men? If I were still trying to please men, I would not be a servant of Christ." —Galatians 1:10

I remember the words of an old Bob Dylan song, "Everybody's gotta please somebody." Well, if you're trying to please your husband or your wife, give it up. It won't work. "What kind of marriage counseling is this?" you say. It's the kind that is based in truth. Human beings are so fickle that what pleases us today may not please us tomorrow. It's like trying to hit a moving target; it's a losing proposition. Let's be real. Has it worked for you? There's a better way, one that works. Live your life, not to please your spouse, or anyone else; live your life to please God. You see, God doesn't change. What pleases Him today will please Him tomorrow. It's a goal much more attainable. Then, if you're loving your spouse in a way that pleases God, chances are your spouse will be pleased, because it will be the love of God expressed through you. Wow! It will be a love directed by your spouses' needs, (not necessarily their wants). It will be a love rooted in the wisdom of God, and energized by the power of his Spirit working in you, a love that transcends human fickleness. Change your focus. Get your sights off of trying to please each other, and fix them on pleasing God with the way you love each other. Everyone will be pleased, and God will get the glory! After all, "Everybody's gotta please somebody." It may as well be the One who can be pleased!

Question for Dialogue: In what ways have we tried to please each other that just never seemed to work? How can we better please God with the way we love and treat each other?

Pray Together: Lord, help us to live for one single purpose: To please you with the way we love and treat each other, so that your love will freely flow through our lives and our home.

#59 Why Haven't I Died Yet Lord?

> *"I have been crucified with Christ. It is no longer I that live, but Christ lives in me...,"* —Galatians 2:20

Do you really want a happy marriage and a successful Christian life? Then follow rule #1 — *Die!* Yep. Die to yourself. But you say, "He said mean and nasty things to me," or "She said hurtful things that made me feel like less than a man." So what! There is only one way that we can triumph over these real feelings of hurt and anger to reconnect with our spouse in a loving, harmonious relationship. I didn't say it was easy. It isn't easy. It's not even natural, but it is worth it, because it's not about us. It's about the Kingdom. Die! Die to self. It's not about you. Haven't we claimed to be crucified with Christ? It is not we who live, but Christ in us? This is where the rubber meets the road, or more precisely, where our flesh meets the Cross. You know, where your will, and His will "cross." Let His light shine on the darkness that it may be crucified. Only then will we be in a position to know reconciliation first with Christ, then with each other. Only then can we be truly "otherly-minded." The good news is you'll be free from pain. You see, you can't hurt a dead man (or woman). Die to self and let Christ rise from within you?

Question for Dialogue: Do you think I take things personal too often? Are we "otherly-minded" or do we get stuck on "self"?

Pray Together: Dear Lord, please help us to die to self, so that we can both be otherly-minded and free to bless others.

#60 You Have an Enemy

"It is to a man's honor to avoid strife, but every fool is quick to quarrel." —Proverbs 20:3

Few principles will enrich your marriage more than the principle of avoiding strife. One of the most important lessons we've learned, that has done more to change our relationship perhaps more than any other, is coming to realize that we are not each other's enemy, but we do have an enemy—*the spirit of strife!* The spirit of strife is on assignment to destroy your marriage. To allow him to be lord in your home is to allow certain disaster. When he is detected husband and wife must close ranks, regardless of internal squabbles to defend against this outside enemy who is sure to cause disorder, anger, resentment, and even hatred when, in fact, that hatred should be directed at him. We must avoid strife at all costs if the marriage is to succeed. It won't matter who's right if there is no marriage. If someone has to win the argument, let it be your spouse. The world won't come to an end! Furthermore, the spirit of strife will be defeated. If you can't let the other win the argument, take a time out. Come back to the issue later when the air isn't so emotionally charged. Do whatever it takes. Just don't let strife take control. The ultimate question is "Who will be lord in your life, the spirit of strife or the Prince of Peace?"

Question for Dialogue: Does the spirit of strife often find its way into our marriage and our home? How can we better avoid it?

Pray Together: Lord, help us to close ranks against this outside enemy so that strife will not have dominion over our marriage and our home.

#61 Are We Ready?

> *"As God's co-workers we urge you not to receive God's grace in vain, for he says, "In the time of my favor I heard you, and in the day of salvation I helped you." I tell you, now is the time of God's favor, now is the day of salvation."*
> —2 Corinthians 6:1-2 (NIV)

This year may very well be a significant year in world history. No one wants to be a "doomsday preacher," but even though we've seen Islamic terrorism as early as the thirteenth century, they never had access to the weapons of mass destruction that they have today, insuring that the next world war is likely to be in our lifetime—it could be today! There are some things we have control over, and some things we don't. We don't have control over world wars or mass destruction, or even a report of terminal cancer. We do however, have control over some things, namely, our minds and our relationships. So let us continue to plan our lives to live to be a hundred and twenty, but let us also be ready to go tonight, by insuring that our relationships are right, first with God, then with those He has put in our lives to love. Let us truly be God's co-workers spreading His love and grace wherever He places us, so that whenever He calls us our lamps will be filled with oil (Matthew 25:10), and we'll step into His chamber. Because in the end (figuratively and literally), what matters is faith expressing itself in love, (Galatians 5:6). For "Now is the Day of Salvation."

Question for Dialogue: Do you think we're ready if Jesus were to come tonight? Are our relationships in right order as far as it is possible with us? (Romans 12:18).

Pray Together: Lord help us to make sober assessment of our readiness, and help us to encourage one another, in love, to work on our relationships to be ready for your coming...whenever it will be. It could be today.

#62 An Overcomer or a "Hanger-Inner?"

"For everyone who is born of God overcomes the world. This is the victory that has overcome the world, even our faith."
—1 John 5:4 (NAS)

Do you really feel confident that you will overcome the problems and challenges to your marriage, or do you feel like the problems are forming into a giant snowball at the top of a mountain above ready to come down at you? Where is this victory that's supposed to overcome the world? As John said, it's our faith, our faith in the person of Jesus Christ. It's knowing that He is in control and even if the snowball comes rolling over me, I'll get right back up and continue my walk with Him. The only thing these problems may accomplish is to validate my share in the Kingdom. Jesus tells us, "To him who overcomes I will give the right to eat of the tree of life..."(Rev. 2:7b) Unfortunately, we can't be overcomers without stuff to overcome. Do our marriage problems look like that snowball coming down that mountain? Then it's time to build our faith. Don't even try to stop that coming snowball, or avalanche, without a solid confidence in His faithfulness to help overcome, anger with kindness, selfishness with grace, anxiety with peace, frustration with hope, and everything else with pure, unadulterated love. Resolve in your own heart to never again answer the question, "How are you?" with the answer, "Hanging in there." You were never called to be a "hanger-inner." You were called to be an overcomer.

Question for Dialogue: Do we feel like overcomers, or do we feel like we're being overcome? Why?

Pray Together: Lord, help us to change our mindset from "hanging in there" to "overcoming," so that what the enemy of our marriage sent to divide us will actually cause us to close ranks against him, as we overcome him together.

#63 LOVE COMPELS

"For Christ's love compels us..."   —2 Corinthians 15:14

The quality of our most important relationships is a function of the small decisions we make continually. "Shall I ask her how her day was, or just go turn on the T.V. and relax?" "Do I get off the phone to greet him at the door when I hear the car pull up?" You see, love is a compelling force that moves us toward one another. Sin is a repelling force that causes us to withdraw into our own comfort zone. I may not want to ask my wife how her day went, because maybe I really just don't care at the moment. After all, I'm tired; I worked all day. I just want to plop my feet up on the ottoman and chill. The wife may not want to cut her phone conversation short with her best friend when she hears his car pull up. After all, she hasn't talked to her friend all week, and there's much to catch up on. If we're going to love each other we need to let Christ's love compel us toward one another precisely when it means sacrifice. There is no love without sacrifice. In fact, love without sacrifice is use. We must be compelled to love even when it means risking conflict. It's Christ's love that compels us to do whatever it takes to draw closer, even when it means dealing with conflict. It's sin that causes us to avoid each other. If we find ourselves being repelled, it's probably not love. Sin repels; love is a compelling force.

Question for Dialogue: When do I feel compelled to come to you; when do I feel repelled to get away from you?

Pray Together: Lord, let your love compel us to be engaged and stay engaged even when we may risk conflict. Keep us from avoiding one another just because it's more comfortable.

#64 Real Climate Change

"Immediately, after the distress of those days "the sun will be darkened, and the moon will not give its light; the stars will fall from the sky, and the heavenly bodies will be shaken."
—Matthew 24:29

Oh, yes, it's certain there will be climate change, but I never cease to be amazed at the sense of self-importance man demonstrates to think that he can control the weather. The sun burps and we have global warming for a spell. It remains quiet and we have a mini-ice age. Yet, human pride finds a sense of self-importance developing theories and arguments that distract him from what he needs to be doing; that is changing the climate in his own home. That's one climate change we do have control over. I'm reminded of the wisdom of Father Washington who said in a letter to his friend, Burwell Bassett, "I have always considered marriage as the most interesting event of one's life, the foundation of happiness or misery." Even George knew the climate in the home could be profound happiness or total misery. Let's quit arguing about climate change "out there" and let's effect climate change in our own homes. Let's establish a climate of righteousness, peace and joy, and no matter what the weather looks like outside, home is where we will want to be.

Question for Dialogue: What is the climate in our home? Is it righteousness, peace and joy, or is it something else? What can we do to change it?

Pray Together: Lord, help us to be mindful of the fact that the climate in our own home is in our own power to control –with your help, of course. Let it be a climate of righteousness, peace and joy.

#65 COCKLES OF YOUR HEART

"May our Lord Jesus Christ himself and God our Father... encourage your hearts and strengthen you in every good deed and word." —2 Thessalonians 2:16, 17

This morning Penny was sitting at the breakfast table feeling somewhat chilly, so I asked her affectionately, "Well Hon, what can I do to warm the cockles of your little heart?" Then I thought, "What in the world are 'the cockles of your heart'?" I realized I had no idea what cockles are, but I guess I must have heard that phrase somewhere, and my warped brain's sense of random retrieval just pulled it out before I realized I had no clue what it means. So we pulled out the American Heritage Dictionary, and this is what it said about cockles: "Any of bivalve mollusks of the family Cardiidae having rounded or heart shaped shells with radiating ribs." Well, that surely didn't help, but then four definitions down after a couple of things about ribs and wrinkles it said, 'one's inner most feelings as in the idiom, 'the cockles of your heart.' That's it! That's what I want to do. I want to warm the little wrinkles in Penny's heart, that innermost place beyond the reach of physical expression. It's spiritual! So we left the breakfast table and headed for the office still somewhat chilled on the outside, but with a new sense of mission and adventure: How can we warm the cockles of one another's hearts? It's OK; it's not a bad word; it's a new challenge.

<u>Question for Dialogue:</u> What are some things that I can do that would make you feel warm inside even when it's cold outside?

<u>Pray Together:</u> Lord, help us to be mindful of ways we can warm the cockles of one another's hearts. Give us the insight, the wisdom, the power and the grace.

#66 Strife Eliminator

"A gentle answer turns away wrath, but a harsh word stirs up anger" —Proverbs 15:1

Here is a strife eliminator you can try using that will disarm that person you can't seem to communicate with because they always get defensive, and you just can't seem to have a civil adult-to-adult conversation about anything with them. Try responding to whatever they say, with: *"You could be right."* You'll be amazed at how quickly their countenance will change, and they may even be in a position to hear your point of view. Why? Because you affirmed them by acknowledging that they could be right. And in fact, that may be the case! Don't ever think you can discount someone's point of view or pronounce them "wrong" before you've had a chance to hear and process what was said. The apostle Paul taught us to be careful when you think you stand lest you fall (1 Corinthians 10:12). They could be right! Communication is often more about our emotions than logic, and saying "You could be right" has the effect of putting you on "their" side emotionally instead of being in an adversarial, or oppositional stance. Then you can have communication. Amos 3:3 says, "How can two walk together lest they be agreed." Try it; it works. And you know what? I could be right!

Question for Dialogue: Do you think I react to you in a way that makes you feel I'm your opponent instead of your partner?

Pray Together: Lord, help us to have the maturity and self-control to acknowledge that our partner just might be right, and we will pause and consider their point of view before we respond.

#67 What Drives You, Faith or Fear?

"For God did not give us a spirit of fear, but of love, joy and a sound mind."   —2 Timothy 1:7 (NKJV)

It seems like the more I study God's word, the more I see that simple principles govern our lives, not some complex theology -principles that are at work whether we believe in them or not. If I walk off the edge of a roof I'm going to fall, whether I believe in gravity or not, because there are certain principles in effect in the physical world, like the principles regarding gravity. There are also spiritual principles that govern at the very core of one's being, like the principle of faith and fear. You see, faith is the power of God as fear is the power of Satan. We're all born with the same ability to believe. However since Satan is the god of this world (2 Cor. 4:4 NAS), it is his lies that the natural man tends to believe. His lies are always negative and fear producing, such as, "You'll get sick," "you'll fail," "you're not good enough," etc. The only antidote for being driven by fear is to put your belief energy into God's truth and turn fear into faith. Each belief system will work to bring into manifestation the object of its own belief. In other words, you'll get whatever you believe, good or bad. (Proverbs 23:7 KJV) Write down the lies of Satan that you have been believing, then study the Scriptures to learn what God says about those very issues, and redirect your belief energy from Satan's lies to God' Truth, and be driven by creative faith instead of destructive fear. *The righteous will live by faith.* -Romans 1:17

<u>**Question for Dialogue**</u>: What lies of Satan have we been believing that cause us to act out of our fears? What is God's Truth?

<u>**Pray Together**</u>: Lord, help us redirect our belief energy from Satan's lies to your truth, that we will be driven by faith, not fear.

#68 Straining Forward

"Brothers, I do not consider myself yet to have taken hold of it. But one thing I do: Forgetting what is behind and straining toward what is ahead, I press on toward the goal to win the prize for which God has called me heavenward in Christ Jesus." —Philippians 3:13-15

Here we had an entire weekend off to get caught up on some housework, recreation and relaxation, and wouldn't you just expect "Ole Beady Eyes" to just try to mess it up by causing some kind of a tiff between us that would ruin the whole weekend? Yeah, you've been there. Don't think that just because we're marriage counselors we never have a bad day. Sometimes I think we're even more sensitive to hurts. Well anyway, Saturday we "had words." There was a time when that would have easily ruined our entire weekend. But instead of running off to our own corners to lick our wounds and fret, we decided to talk it through. And you know what? Though it was still difficult to stay in that place of grace, without letting emotions sabotage the dialogue, with the help of the Holy Spirit we were able to "strain" forward, and end of our conversation, with prayer, and a little better understanding of each other, and a little stronger in our "oneness" as God is building us up into Him. On Sunday, we awakened to a beautiful Spring-like day. All of nature seemed to worship God. We took a picnic lunch and visited John Jay's homestead in Westchester. It was beautiful. As we strolled the grounds hand-in-hand we really felt like we were winning the prize for which God had called us heavenward in Christ Jesus. Even if Saturday was difficult. It was a strain, but it was a strain forward.

Question for The Both of Us: How has the enemy caused us to sabotage weekends or vacations that should have been a real blessed time? How did each one of us contribute to the disaster?

Prayer For The Both of Us: Lord, help us to have the gentleness and self-control to strain forward no matter how difficult it may be. Help us to redeem the times so that Ole Beady Eyes will not steal the good times you have reserved for us.

#69 When Bad Things Happen

> *"His wife said to him, "Are you still maintaining your integrity? Curse God and die!" He replied, "You are talking like a foolish woman. Shall we accept good from God, and not trouble?"*   —Job 2:9, 10

Job's counselors and his wife were no different than today's critics. Human nature doesn't change. (So much for evolution!). With tragedies like mass shootings, and natural disasters ruining lives, it's only natural for one to question the reality of a good God.

The truth is that God has allowed evil to have limited dominion in this fallen world, so we have both good and evil. The Scriptures tell us "the rain falls on the just and the unjust." When tragedy strikes, whoever is in the way gets it. The only advantage a believer has is the indwelling Holy Spirit—power to overcome adversity that a non-believer doesn't have. Penny and I are going through a season of physical challenges, but we know it's part of the deal, so we keep our eyes, and our minds on the blessings we've been given as we work to overcome the physical challenges. It's been said that everyone wants to go to heaven but nobody wants to die. Well, I'm sorry; it just doesn't work that way. If we want to be raised with Him we must also be willing to suffer with Him, (2 Tim. 2:12).So what do we do in the face of challenge or tragedy? We hang on to each other and Jesus and count our blessings until the difficulties are overcome We come out the other side stronger, more in love with each other and Jesus, and we've grown just a little bit more in our Christian character. We have been refined, yet once again.

Question for Dialogue: How do we do when it comes to accepting both blessings and troubles? Do when tend to go through difficult times feeling alone or do we go through them together?

Pray Together: Lord, help us to overcome troubles by leaning on you and each other, so that we can accept both blessings and troubles, and become a stronger witness as a Christian couple.

#70 Learning to Love

"For in Christ Jesus neither circumcision nor uncircumcision has any value. The only thing that counts is faith expressing itself through love." —Galatians 5:6

What I find interesting is the fact that the more I learn about our faith, the simpler the message becomes. It's summed up in Paul's teaching that the only thing that matters is a faith expressed in love. That's it! In other words, this entire earthly sojourn is about one thing—*learning to love*. In fact, marriage is the primary instrument God uses to teach us to love. That's why it's quite often the most difficult relationship one might have. You see, it's easy to put on the Christian face on Sunday in church. You may have even learned to control your behavior in the work place, but the real you is demonstrated by the way you treat your spouse at home. Is it with selfless tender-hearted kindness, or is it with impatience, annoyance and a selfish agenda? Here is the test. Look at the way you treat your spouse, and measure your love by that gauge. For those who aren't married, substitute your most difficult relationship. Have you learned to love? Are you learning to love? Forget about the "religious stuff." It all comes down to one thing: Are you learning to love? Remember, your faith—or lack thereof—is expressed in the way you love. How are you doing?

Question for Dialogue: Have you seen me grow in love? How? Can you be more specific?

Pray Together: Lord, please help us to grow in love with you first, then with one another, so that in the love we have demonstrated for each other, the world will see Jesus.

#71 Q-TIP THERAPY

"Great peace have they which love thy law: and nothing shall offend them." —Psalm 119:165 (KJV)

Wouldn't you just love to be in that place where nothing will offend you, where no one can rock your boat. You can. Just Quit Taking It Personal! Call it Q-TIP Therapy. (Q.T.I.P.)

In fact, carry one or two Q Tips with you and when you hear your spouse getting offended don't say a word. Just hand them a Q-Tip, and laugh about it –Don't Fight! If we're going to call ourselves Christians, we ought to be practicing the most fundamental element of our faith –self denial. What did Jesus say?

"If anyone would come after me, he must deny himself and take up his cross daily and follow me." –Luke 9:23

In other words, it's not about you, so quit taking it personal! Have a Q-TIP!

Question for Dialogue: Do you think I take things personally? Do you think I would be offended if you handed me a Q-Tip? Would you be offended if I handed you one?

Pray Together: Lord, help us to be true disciples of Christ by using Q-TIP Therapy that you might be glorified in our relationship.

#72 CHANGE

"Therefore, if anyone is in Christ, he is a new creation; the old has gone, the new has come!" —2 Corinthians 5:17

It's been said that the only one who like change is a wet baby. Most of us don't welcome unexpected change. But change will come whether we expect it or not. The real issue is, "What kind of change, do we want?" The question applies to our marriages just as much as it does to politics. The good news is that we can choose the kind of change we want. The bad news is that if we don't choose favorable change, unfavorable change will happen all by itself, disproving, once again, the theory of evolution. If we aren't proactive, and purposefully making changes in our marriages, and in our lives, to bring more love, more communication and more oneness, we will naturally see changes that will produce more indifference, more strife and more isolation. Things don't get better by themselves. In fact, over time, without intelligent intervention, there will be slow, but certain, dissolution of relationships. It's natural. It's the spirit of this world. The good news is we can choose to change every day to be a little more like Christ. Every day our marriages can reflect more of His love. Every day we can grow in love, peace and oneness, and God will get the glory. That's the only change you can believe in. Make a choice. Choose to change one thing today.

Question for Dialogue: Have changes in our marriage been good? What is one thing we can work on changing today?

Pray Together: Lord, help us to choose to make good changes that will help us grow together and not apart.

#73 GRATEFUL OR GRUMBLER?

"Be joyful always; pray continually; give thanks in all circumstances, for this is God's will for you in Christ Jesus."
— 1 Thessalonians. 5:16-18

One of the classic "oldies" from my Brooklyn teeny-bopper days declared, "There are just two kinds of people in the world. They are a boy and girl." That's at least partially true. Yes, there are just two kinds of people in the world, but they are the "grateful and the grumblers." You see, we all have things that God has given us and done for us, as well as things He hasn't given us, or done for us. But whether we walk in joy or misery depends on which of these two realities we dwell in. If I continually think of all that God has given me, and done in my life, I develop a heart of gratitude and a fountain of joy! However, if I dwell on all that God hasn't given me, or done for me, I develop a grumbling heart, eventually turning into a bitter pool. Every word is a complaint or criticism, and nobody likes a complainer. The good news is that we can live in joy by choosing to dwell on all that God has given us and done for us. We're not denying the negatives, but we're not allowing them to dwell in our minds. I'm living in the positives. That's my mental address. The more I dwell there, the more grateful and joyful I become. That's the abundant life Jesus spoke of! There are just two kinds of people in the world –the grateful and the grumblers. I've chosen to be in the first group. We have a lot to be thankful for. Let's be counted among the grateful.

Question for Dialogue: Do you see me as one of the "grateful" or one of the "grumblers"? Can you explain?

Pray Together: Lord, help us to dwell in what you have given us and what you have done for us. Keep our mental address focused on your goodness.

#74 The Liberty of Love

"Each man should give what he has decided in his heart to give, not reluctantly or under compulsion. For God loves a cheerful giver." —2 Corinthians 9:7

Even though Paul was talking specifically about money in his letter to the believers in Corinth, he reveals a deeper principle that should be foundational to every area of our lives. We can call it, "the spirit of giving." What greater gift can we give than the gift of love? And love, to be love, must be freely given, without condition or expectation of anything in return. We must want to sacrifice for the needs of the other person, because we want to see that person blessed, not because we want something for ourselves. If our motive is to receive something in return, it's no longer love; it's mutual use. Attempting to love from a sense of duty or obligation leads to nothing but resentment and frustration. The only cure is a heart transplant. We must ask God to remove our heart of self-centeredness and replace it with His heart of selflessness. This is the spirit of giving. Only then will we be able to "freely" love, because it will be God's love freely given to us, so that we will be able to pass on to our spouse. That is the liberty of love.

Question for Dialogue: Do you feel like my love for you is freely given, or do you feel like I expect something in return?

Prayer for the Both of Us: Lord, help us to love freely, not out of compulsion or obligation, but without condition or expectation. Help us to love as You have loved us.

#75 WHEN IT'S MATHEMATICALLY IMPOSSIBLE!

"Who are you to judge someone else's servant? To their own master, servants stand or fall. And they will stand, for the Lord is able to make them stand." —Romans 14:4

So let's pose a mathematical question: If the husband is waiting for the wife to change, and the wife is waiting for the husband to change, how long will it take before we see any change? Yep, you got it—*never!* Yet, that is often the situation we see in the counseling room where each spouse is waiting for the other to change, and it always ends up in a stalemate which sometimes lasts for years! It's not until each one gets their eyes off the other and starts to take a sober assessment of themselves that we begin to see change. Someone has to break the deadlock, and it's most often the husband who must initiate love differently before he can see a change in the wife's response. The good news is that once the deadlock is broken things begin to move as both begin to look at themselves to see how they are falling short of God's plans and purpose for their own lives as God teaches them to love. Then they realize they are both on this journey together; both are growing and even straining forward for the prize of seeing the vision they once had for their marriage restored and renewed.

Question for Dialogue: Do you think you might be waiting for me to change before you think about making changes in yourself?

Pray Together: Lord, help us to break the stalemate by getting our eyes off each other and looking to you to change us right where we are.

#76 LET'S TALK ADULT-TO-ADULT

> *"Be devoted to one another in love. Honor one another above yourselves."* —Romans 12:10

In a sense, we all have three distinct personalities within us that were developed in our childhood. First, is the *"parent"* in all of us that was formed by the way we heard our parents speak to us in an authoritative voice like "you need to do better," or "you need to pick up your clothes," etc. Any time you can visualize a finger pointing, it's coming from the parent in us. There is a place for that—when speaking to our children. Then you have the *"child"* in us that was developed by the way we reacted to our parents, and is driven by emotions. We cried, we yelled; we ran into our room and shut the door. However we reacted, it was emotionally driven. Then we have the *"adult"* that is characterized by a sense of mutual respect. No one is talking "down" to anyone. We're speaking across to one another, adult-to-adult without charged emotion. This is typically what we see in the counseling room. The problem is that the only place where effective communication happens is when we're in the *adult-to-adult* mode. The challenge then, is to come down out of our *"parent"* or up out of our *"child"* to have meaningful and effective communication. Yes, it takes maturity and self-control, but without *adult-to-adult* communication nothing gets resolved. We just keep arguing about the same ole things. So, let's be adults!

<u>Question for Dialogue</u>: Do we speak to one another out of our *"parent,"* our *"child,"* or out of our *"adult"*?

<u>Pray Together:</u> Lord, help us to have the self-control to come down out of our *"parent"* or up out of our *"child"* so we can communicate *"adult-to-adult."*

Special Days and Seasons

*There is a time for everything,
and a season for every activity under the heavens:
a time to be born and a time to die,
a time to plant and a time to uproot,
a time to kill and a time to heal,
a time to tear down and a time to build,
a time to weep and a time to laugh,
a time to mourn and a time to dance,
a time to scatter stones and a time to gather them,
a time to embrace and a time to refrain from embracing,
a time to search and a time to give up,
a time to keep and a time to throw away,
a time to tear and a time to mend,
a time to be silent and a time to speak,
a time to love and a time to hate,
a time for war and a time for peace."*
—Ecclesiastes 3:1-8

*"He changes times and seasons; he deposes kings
and raises up others. He gives wisdom to the wise
and knowledge to the discerning."*
—Daniel 2:21

Winter

*"Then came the Festival of Dedication at Jerusalem.
It was winter and Jesus was in the temple courts walking in
Solomon's Colonnade."*
—John 10:22, 23

#77 Break the Curse

> "...I, the LORD your God, am a jealous God, punishing the children for the sin of the fathers to the third and fourth generation...but showing love to a thousand generations of those who love me..." --Exodus 20:5-6

As we prepare for Christmas we might ask, "What's the best gift I can give my children?" Sure, we'll listen to the children to hear what they want after they've been brain-washed by the advertisers, then we'll go on the hunt until we find it. But ask, "How have these gifts really benefited my child?" Truth be told, our children are living under the curse of fathers who have not followed Christ. This curse remains, "to the third and fourth generation." As each generation continues to turn their hearts against Christ, the curse continues until someone puts a stop to it by choosing to turn to God. God promises that He will show love to a thousand generations to those who would love Him. The challenge is to choose whether we will we go on buying gifts that have no real benefit for our children, or give a gift that will deliver them from the curse. What is that gift? --Parents who love God, and demonstrate it by their lifestyle. There are just some things you can't buy with a Visa Card. What will we give our children this Christmas, more meaningless toys, or the love of God? The choice, as always, is in our hands, and in our hearts.

Question for Dialogue: What are we passing on to our children this Christmas? Are we perpetuating the curse, or demonstrating the love of God in our home and in our relationships?

Pray Together: Lord, help us give to break the curse and give our children the best gift ever—the love of God.

#78 Not Fake News

"And Mary said: 'My soul glorifies the Lord and my spirit rejoices in God my Savior, for he has been mindful of the humble state of his servant. From now on all generations will call me blessed, or the Mighty One has done great things for me—holy is his name.'" —Luke 1:46-49

Thank God that in this world of "Fake News" we know of an unbelievable truth that has changed the course of mankind for over 2,000 years and is still changing the course of lives of people every day, people who are searching for peace in a world of chaos. The miracle that Mary experienced is for all of us. She was the first to carry the Christ child, Jesus who is the way to eternal and abundant life. He died and rose from the dead to prove He was the real deal. Ever since then, Christ has been born in the hearts of millions who were willing to surrender their lives for the life Christ has to offer. Only then, can one truly know the love of God, and have that love to give to another. Without Christ, the best a couple can have is a mutual use agreement. That isn't love, and it just doesn't work. Yes, some people who are not Christians do have a genuine love, but that isn't the norm. Theologians call that "prevenient grace," the acts of God working in the lives of people who don't know Him. The only way one can be assured of knowing love is to give your life to Jesus, and let Him give you His unconditional love. The secret for a successful marriage is no secret at all—it is Jesus. As we consider the season of Christmas let's seriously consider allowing the Christ Child who was born to Mary more than 2,000 years ago be born again in our own hearts today. This is one reality you can count on; it is not "fake news," *thank God!*

Question for Dialogue: Have you had the Christ child born in your own heart? How has that changed your outlook? Your life?

Pray Together: Lord, help us to sing Mary's song from the heart, glorifying God and rejoicing in what He is doing in our lives.

#79 How Joseph Loved Mary

"...but before they came together she was found to be with child through the Holy Spirit. Because Joseph, her husband was a righteous man and did not want to expose her to public disgrace, he had in mind to divorce her quietly."
—Matthew 1:18, 19

Here he was "betrothed" (For all practical purposes, that's being legally married without the physical union.), and then she comes with this story that she was pregnant, not by another man, but by the Holy Spirit! Yeah, right? What was Joseph's reaction? Did he say, "How could you do this to me?" Did he get all offended? "He had a right to" you say. Perhaps, but love has nothing to do with rights. The Bible tells us that he was more concerned with Mary's well-being than he was with his rights, or even his own hurt. He sought to protect her, and if there must be a divorce let it be done quietly so as not to humiliate her. You see, love is always otherly-minded. Love doesn't accuse, even when it's based in fact. "Love covers a multitude of sins" (Proverbs 10:12). Joseph loved Mary by his protective actions. And this was all before the Angel appeared to him to tell him that Mary wasn't lying. The baby in her womb really was conceived by the Holy Spirit! And so, Joseph had the honor of parenting God's only Son. This Christmas season let us purpose in our own hearts not to take offense, not to accuse, but rather to protect and to minister the grace of God to one another, and see what miracle God can birth in each and every one of us this Christmas season.

Question for Dialogue: Do we love and protect one another unconditionally, or do we get offended at the slightest provocation?

Pray Together: Lord help us to love as Joseph loved, not counting our sins against one another, but rather protecting and seeking the well-being of one another.

#80 Wise Couples Still Seek Him

> *"— from the east came Wise men to Jerusalem and asked, 'Where is the one who has been born king of the Jews? We saw his star in the east and have come to worship him.'"*
> –Matthew 2:1, 2

I recently had a conversation with someone who was obviously possessed by the spirit of Scrooge, because he complained about Christmas being such an interruption in his life messing up business for a month. I felt sad, because though I understood where he was coming from, I could see he was missing the bigger picture—*God with us!* Think of the Wise Men. They interrupted their lives, not for a month, but for two years to seek Him. They no doubt had their personality issues, but they were able to put them aside for the greater cause –to pursue Him! This is the time of year to put our differences aside and pursue Christ with a passion that will allow His perfect love to displace our fears and insecurities, and to burn in us in a way that would be apparent to all. Though our sin may be red as scarlet, we will see only white as snow, (Isaiah 1:18). The Bible teaches that the fool says in his heart there is no God, but wise men will seek Him. The choice is clear: Will we live in a way that discounts God, or will we pursue Him with all that is within us –even if it is an interruption. Foolish or wise, what will it be? As always the choice is ours –the power is His.

Question for Dialogue: Are we diligently seeking the fullness of Christ this Christmas?

Pray Together: Lord, help us to interrupt whatever schedules we may have had to pursue Christ this special season.

#81 Christmas and Marriage

"This is how the birth of Jesus Christ came about: His mother Mary was pledged to be married to Joseph, but before they came together, she was found to be with child through the Holy Spirit." —Matthew 1:18

Think about it. Jesus could have chosen to come into our world in so many different ways. He could have come from nowhere, simply appearing out of the desert, maybe walking out of a burning bush like the one He used to talk to Moses from. He could have come down majestically out of the sky led by a brigade of heavenly chariots. But God chose to wait until Joseph betrothed Mary, and then He blessed that betrothal with the seed of The Savior of mankind. If marriage is that special to God, shouldn't it be special to us? The greatest gift we can give to our children this Christmas is the gift of a loving Mom and Dad who esteem highly the institution of marriage, and who demonstrate the love of Christ in holy matrimony. By the love we demonstrate one for another our children will know we are His disciples. This Christmas let's give the gift of a renewed commitment to love as Christ loved us –selflessly, and to do whatever it takes to make our marriage all that God wants it to be. It won't cost you a penny, but it will cost all you have to deny yourself for the well-being of another. That's what marriage is. It's not 50-50; it's 100-100! Is it impossible? You bet. That's why we serve a God of miracles who makes the impossible possible, beginning in our hearts.

Question for Dialogue: What kind of a gift are we giving our children this year? Is it a loving, Christ-filled marriage, evident to all?

Pray Together: Lord, help us to give to our children the very best gift possible. Let them see a marriage filled with the love of Christ.

#82 Rejoice With Truth (New Years)

"Love does not delight in evil but it rejoices with the truth."
— 1 Corinthians 13:6

Isn't it interesting how Paul doesn't contrast evil with good in this passage, but rather, he contrasts it with truth. On the one hand you have evil, and on the other, you have truth. That's because truth is good. "But the truth of my situation isn't so good," you say. "In fact, the truth of my situation is pretty lousy!" I hear you. But let's start the New Year with the understanding that no matter what your situation looks like, you're only seeing part of it. Truth goes beyond what you see. Truth has a name -Jesus! He said, "I am the Way, the Truth, and the Life," (John 14:6). To the extent that your situation is in Jesus, it is good! Please don't be one of those "normal" people who are limited by what you see. Truth goes beyond the visible. That's why it's good! No matter what you see, Jesus really is able to bring it to a good report. He really is able to take our mess, and do something beautiful with it -if we'll only let Him. That's why we can always rejoice with the Truth, -with Jesus! Love doesn't focus on the current situation, but on Jesus. He is the One who can provide what we need, who can lift us up when we're down, who can give us the love we need for each other -a love we just don't have in the natural.

Question for Dialogue: Do we really believe, and live life in a way that looks beyond our circumstances to see the Truth—Jesus, in all we do?

Pray Together: Lord, help us to keep our eyes on Jesus, the Author and Finisher of our faith. He is the Truth that is greater than our circumstances.

#83 New Year's "Repentolutions"

> *"I have not come to call the righteous, but sinners to repentance."*   —Luke 5:32

Why not try something different this New Year. Instead of making resolutions that you know you probably won't keep for more than a week, why not try making *"repentolutions?"* That's right. Spend some time with the Lord with pen and paper, and ask Him about the things He would like you to change to better reflect His nature and His character. Then write them all down as they come. Don't spend time trying to analyze them; just write them down as they come to your mind.

Then afterward, you can put them in some kind of order: the more do-able first, then on down the line. If you're really daring you can ask your spouse what he or she sees that needs repentance. Your spouse knows you better than anyone else, and God will probably speak through your spouse more than anyone else. (Why else do you think that's the person you may have the most problem with?)

Then put that list in your wallet or purse and start working on it. Then next year you can test yourself and see how much progress you've made. That's what Christian growth and spiritual formation is all about. So this New Year, instead of resolutions let's make some *"repentolutions."* Happy New Year!

Question for Dialogue: What are some of the things each one of us needs to repent of in this New Year? (Be honest, but full of grace.)

Pray Together: Lord, help us both to take an honest look at the issues we know we need to repent of, and help us to encourage one another as we both seek to change day-by-day.

#84 Vision For the New Year

"Where there is no revelation the people cast off restraint, but blessed is he who keeps the law" —Proverbs 29:18

Do you realize that you've never gone anywhere without first having a vision of that place in your mind? Oh sure, you may have found yourself in places without first seeing them, but that certainly wasn't part of a plan. That was happenstance. The question we need to ask as we begin this new year is, "Will we let life just happen this year and see where we end up, especially in our marriage, or will we seek a vision?" Without a vision you never know if you're on course, because you don't even know where the course is! Anxieties don't come from being off course; they come from not knowing where the course is! Don't live your life by accident this year. Seek God for a vision for your marriage and your life. What does God desire in this new year? More quality time? Better control of your finances? More time with the children? More sex? Whatever it is, seek a vision together. Write it down. Pray about it. Then be "doers" as God enables you. You may not see the entire vision fulfilled, but at least you'll be headed in the right direction. Otherwise, take my word for it, you will go in the wrong direction. Let's not live this new year by happenstance. Let's seek God's vision and be restrained by what that vision calls for, and the new year will be a year of greater glory –His glory!

Question for Dialogue: What do you think the Lord has for us in this new year? What goals would you like to see accomplished?

Pray Together: Lord, grant us a vision that we might see what your desire is for us in this new year.

#85 Valentine's Day and Marriage

> *"My lover spoke and said to me, 'Arise, my darling, my beautiful one, and come with me'"* — Song of Songs 2:10

When did Valentine's Day begin? One legend contends that Valentine was a Roman priest who served during the third century. When Emperor Claudius II decided that single men made better soldiers than married men, he outlawed marriage to keep his crop of potential soldiers. Valentine, seeing this injustice, defied Claudius and continued performing marriages for young lovers in secret. When Valentine's actions were discovered, Claudius ordered that he be put to death. Other stories suggest that Valentine may have been killed for attempting to help Christians escape harsh Roman prisons where they were often beaten and tortured. There are many, even today, who devalue the sacred institution of marriage. Turn on the TV any day of the week and you'll see romance and sex with everyone but a married couple. It's time to recapture the romance, the excitement, the ecstasy (the real thing), that comes from enjoying the most sacred institution God has given to mankind. As our marriage goes, so goes our relationship with our Maker. The opposite is true as well. As we renew our relationship with God, our marriage is also renewed. Love and marriage is a God thing. So today, as Valentine did, let's fight for our marriages; let's celebrate, enjoy and defend the greatest institution God has given to his human creation.

Question for Dialogue: How can we make Valentine's Day just a little more special this year?

Pray Together: Lord, help us to be determined to fight for our marriage and let the world know this is a sacred institution.

Spring

"See! The winter is past;
the rains are over and gone.
Flowers appear on the earth;
the season of singing has come,
the cooing of doves is heard in our land.
The fig tree forms its early fruit;
the blossoming vines spread their fragrance.
Arise, come, my darling;
my beautiful one, come with me."
—Solomon 2:12, 13

#86 Prepare For the Storm

"When the storm has swept by, the wicked are gone, but the righteous stand firm forever" —Proverbs 10:25

Here we are in the first week of March, and the weather forecast is calling for the biggest snowstorm in decades. Talk about March coming in like a lion! Well, I guess we have to accept the fact that we can't control the weather. But we can control how we make it through by being sure we're prepared. You know, stock up on groceries, flashlight batteries, bottled water, etc.

Relationships are much the same. Storms come up at the most inconvenient times. Unfortunately, we haven't yet invented Doppler radar to foresee storms in relationships. But if you stop to think about it, there may be ways you can observe the atmospheric conditions in the relationship, and predict, with some degree of accuracy, a coming storm. Then again, maybe the storm comes out of nowhere, totally unforeseen or unexpected. Whether we can see it coming or not, the key to making it through the storm is all about preparation. Are we sufficiently joined together in prayer? Are we open and honest with one another about our thoughts and feelings so that no whirlwind in our minds will conjure up vane or hurtful imaginations? Have we made sufficient deposits into one another's love bank so that our account balance will endure the toughest of storms? Are we clothed in the righteousness of Christ, together, where we can find shelter from the storm?

Question for Dialogue: Do you think we're ready to handle the next storm that might come our way? How can we be better prepared?

Pray Together: Lord, help us to be intentional about building up our marriage so that we will be prepared for any storm that might come our way.

#87 Through the Storm

"Without warning, a furious storm came up on the lake, so that the waves swept over the boat." —Matthew 8:24-27

The "storm of the decade" the weather prognosticators warned us about last week never happened. Thank God! Nevertheless, there were many storms, not outside, but inside the homes of couples and families struggling to find a sense of peace and order for their lives. But instead, they often find themselves like the waves of a storm-tossed sea driven, every which way. No peace!

The disciples were actually with Jesus when a storm came, and they reacted as many of us would—in fear. We may express our fear in anger, or depression. Actually, depression is really just anger turned inward. If we react in anger we simply feed the storm and it grows in intensity until it blows us away. During a 48-hour weekend, according to latest statistics, 6,000 families in our nation have succumbed to the storm, and have drowned in divorce. What's the answer? How do we make it through the storms of strife, anger, frustration and fear? Hebrews 6:19 tells us: *"We have this hope as an anchor for the soul, firm and secure."* The key is to be anchored securely in Christ. Regardless of what may be in the wind and the waves, ride it out in grace and truth. It will pass, and you will be on firm ground again, if you are anchored in Him. He is the shelter.

Question for Dialogue: Are we sufficiently anchored in Christ to make it through any storm that may come?

Pray Together: Lord, help us to be anchored in you so that no storm of life will cause us to be blown off the course you have set for us.

#88 After the Storm

> *"He stilled the storm to a whisper; the waves of the sea were hushed."* —Psalm 107:29

Every adversity has the seed of a greater benefit. When the storms come—and they will—and after we have done all we can to be prepared, and after, by His grace, we make it through to the other side, what are we left with? Are we left with a greater sense of division, brokenness, disappointment and anger brought on by the storm, or is there more oneness, a deeper intimacy, a greater love, because we went through the storm together? We have been through some pretty tough storms in our marriage, but the one thing we have purposed in our hearts is to go through the storms together. No longer do we want to isolate from one another, because we're too proud to admit we need each other. No longer do we insist on making it through "on our own." We need Jesus. We need each other. After the storm, when the winds have died down, and the waves have settled, we can look back to see what of our carnal nature God has washed away in the storm. We can allow Jesus to bring healing to both of us. Then we can celebrate the very fact that we made it through, and we're just a little more like Jesus after the storm then we were before.

Question for Dialogue: How did we make it through the last storm? What good has come out of such a stormy time in our marriage?

Pray Together: Lord help us to see the good that has come from the stormy period of our lives that have caused us to grow in Christ.

#89 An Interesting Fast (Lent)

"When words are many, sin is not absent, but he who holds his tongue is wise." —Proverbs 10:19

"You can't fire me; I quit!" are the famous last words of an individual who has to prove to themselves that they matter. The problem is that the self-affirming last word doesn't accomplish anything to resolve the issue or maintain relationship. It just satisfies the ego (**E**asing **G**od **O**ut), a need to establish oneself as the supreme judge who will declare the final verdict. Since this is the traditional season of Lent, let me suggest an interesting fast for those who would have the courage: Try fasting the last word. I guarantee it will change the very nature of your communication and your relationship. The first thing you'll notice will be a new ability to listen to your spouse more attentively, because you won't be thinking about what you're going to say when they finish talking. You'll actually let them have the last word! And guess what? The world won't come to an end! And in the final analysis, you'll find a new ability to listen, understand and communicate effectively. Try it; I dare you! Fast "The Last Word."

Question for Dialogue: Do you think I always need to get that self-affirming last word in?

Pray Together: Lord, help us to have the humility and the self-control to give up that self-affirming last word so we can listen to understand just a little better.

#90 Resurrection and Marriage

"I want to know Christ and the power of his resurrection"
–Philippians 3:10

Jesus Christ was the only man to have ever accurately predicted his own death and resurrection and live to tell about it! The very essence of our faith is wrapped up in this single event. But for the resurrection, Christianity would be just one more religion to help us live in peace and harmony. But if He really was raised from the dead, then He really was who He said He was –God in the flesh! Everything He said and taught would have to be true, including what He said about love and marriage. The apostle, Paul told us to have the mind of Christ, who did not count equality with God something to be grasped, but rather emptied himself, surrendering all his rights, becoming a servant even to death on a cross, and then God gave Him the Name above every name. (Philippians 2). This is the key to knowing Christ and the power of His resurrection. It is surrendering our rights and "crucifying" the self-life. By its very definition there can be no resurrection unless there is first a death, the death of the self-life. This Resurrection season is a time to renew our identification with His crucifixion as we die to self, and any sense of entitlement. Then we can experience the power of the resurrection in our lives and in our marriages, and we can do it today!

Question for Dialogue: Do you think I have sufficiently put to death my self-will, so that the life of Christ can be seen in me?

Pray Together: Lord, help us to put to death any sense of self-will or entitlement that the life of Christ might be seen in our marriage.

#91 Spring Clean Up

"You were taught, with regard to your former way of life, to put off your old self, which is being corrupted by its deceitful desires; to be made new in the attitude of your minds; and to put on the new self, created to be like God in true righteousness and holiness." —Ephesians 4:22-24

Time for Spring cleanup, beginning with ourselves and our marriages. Time to put away the old rubbish in our minds, selfish, and self-centered thoughts of getting what we want, or what we think we deserve. (Believe me, you really don't want what you deserve!) Throw all that mental junk out where the light of God's love can show it to us plainly, then let the blood of Christ wash it away as we repent and choose to renew our minds and walk in newness of life. It's been said that sunlight is the best disinfectant. When it comes to our personal walk with the Lord, and marriage, "Son" light is the only disinfectant. (1 John 1:7,8). Join hands, pray together, ask God to help you both stay focused on the promises of a new season of growth looking forward to a harvest of righteousness. Get rid of all bitterness, contempt and self-centeredness and bask in the warmth of the "Son." It's a wonderful new season. It is the Day of the Lord! Enjoy it!

Question for Dialogue: What's some of the junk that needs to be confessed, brought into the light, and thrown out!

Pray Together: Lord, help us to take an honest look at what needs to be brought into the light and thrown out, so we can clean up our marriage.

#92 Mother's Day

"She watches over the affairs of her household and does not eat the bread of idleness. Her children arise and call her blessed." –Proverbs 31:27,28

There is no one on the face of this earth –no president, no king, no C.E.O., no leader, religious or otherwise who is more worthy of praise and honor than the mother of my children. She is the one who demonstrates unconditional love; she is the one who looks past the faults to see the needs; she is the one who demonstrates forgiveness, seventy times seven. She is the one who believes in you, even when you doubt yourself. Whenever I consider what the love of God looks like here in the earth I see the heart of my children's mother. It is divine; it is supernatural; it is God! As a husband and father, I've come to learn that the emotional bond between Mom and the children is so strong that whatever the children experience is felt by Mom. So when I'm harsh to the children Mom feels the hurt. When I'm loving to the children Mom feels loved. It's no wonder Jesus compared himself to a Mom when He said, "Jerusalem, Jerusalem, how often I have longed to gather your children together, as a hen gathers her chicks under her wings," (Luke 13:34) Mothers are compassion personified. Though we may pray to "Our Father," the answer to our prayers is often seen in that godly woman we call Mother. It can never be emphasized enough just how much mothers bring to our everyday lives the compassion and power of Christ. For showing us Jesus, we honor you!

Special Prayer for Mom: Lord, bless Mom in every possible way as we celebrate Mother's Day. Fill her with your peace and joy, and help me to be a blessing to her, even more than I was last year.

#93 Why Remember? (Memorial Day)

"This is my commandment that you love one another just as I have loved you. Greater love has no one than this, that one lay down his life for his friends." —Jesus (John 15:12, 13)

What does Memorial Day have to do with my marriage? Lots! You see, marriage is based on a commitment to love. The American soldier exemplifies that love when he risks everything so that you and I might know freedom –even his life! We can learn from them. I spent four years in the Air Force during the Viet Nam Era. We were married only eight months when I had to leave for Korea, not to return to my new bride for 13 months. God kept me safe while I lost friends in Viet Nam. Honoring them reminds me of the real nature of love. It's not a feeling or having someone in my life to meet all my needs or wants. It's giving all that I have without guarantee, or expectation of getting anything in return. When I enlisted, some were running off to Canada because they weren't prepared to give -to love. Today, in the same way, many husbands and wives run off to their own places of escape to avoid giving their reasonable service because it calls for sacrifice. We need to be men and women of courage. We need to be prepared to give no matter the cost. When we look at the flag the red stripes reminds us of the blood that flowed to win our freedom, not just on the battlefields of war, but also on Calvary's hill to win our freedom from sin, hell, death and the grave. We are free to love, because of those who went before us, loving us, purchasing our freedom with their lives, including, and especially, the Son of God. Let's remember and commit to carrying on the tradition of loving no matter the cost. We can do no less.

Question for Dialogue: Do we do enough to honor those who gave their lives for our freedom, especially Jesus!

Pray Together: Lord, help us never to lose sight or appreciation for those who gave their lives so that we might be free: Jesus Christ and the American soldier.

Summer

*"Now learn this lesson from the fig tree:
As soon as its twigs get tender and its leaves come out,
you know that summer is near."* —Matthew 24:32

#94 FATHER'S DAY

"For this reason I kneel before the Father, from whom his whole family in heaven and on earth derives its name."
—Ephesians 3:14

The Bible tells us that God's entire family, in heaven and in earth derives its name from "Father." And yet, God trusts us to share His Name with us. What an awesome privilege, and yet what a great responsibility! We see all of God's creative order beginning and flowing out of the word, "Father." When we reflect the nature and character of our Heavenly Father all is in right order; we enjoy fullness of joy and life more abundantly. When we do not reflect the nature of God we see every kind of dysfunction and disorder. Why do you think our pop culture always makes a point of denigrating the role of the Father? It's because the spirit that drives pop culture (evolution, secular humanism, etc.,) is anti-God and anti-Creation. All of Creation derives from the "Fatherhood" of God. It is from our Father in heaven that we find the source of our very existence, not some primordial slime that drifted out of the ocean. As we celebrate Father's Day let us again lift fatherhood to its rightful place of prominence so that we will see order, peace and prosperity in the lives of our own children, and even in our nation. We can do it, if we will kneel before our Father to receive His heart of love and courage. It's a great privilege, and an awesome responsibility. Let's do it.

Question for Dialogue: Do we take the office of "Father" seriously enough to be fully engaged in family life, and lead in love?

Pray Together: Lord, help us to step up to the plate to fulfill our duties as a Father, and help us truly lead in love by your example.

#95 Her Perspective on Father's Day

> *"But I want you to understand That Christ is the head of every man, and the man is the head of the woman, and God is the head of Christ."*
> —1 Corinthians 11:3

We just celebrated Father's Day. Although many homes are without a natural father, we can be grateful that we all have a perfect Heavenly Father, someone who cares for us, and is bigger than you and me. The role of husband and father is a difficult one. It's up to them to figure out what God's will is for this family and lead the way by example. Think about your husband. Do you sometimes feel resentful because he seems to think he only has to go to work, and that's where his responsibility ends? Do you often feel like you have to do everything else? I understand, but you know it really is tough out there, "on the job." They need our help, encouragement, support and prayers as much as we need theirs. Does your husband feel honored by the way you treat him, or does he feel like just one of the kids, or even worse, someone that is just there for the paycheck? Have you spent time with the Lord interceding for God's gift to you- -your companion, your lover and friend? Do you ask your husband, "How can I pray for you?" You see, it's really not about us, or them, or even our children. It is about God! It is a Kingdom issue.

<u>Question for me</u>: Am I a woman of God in my home? In my heart? In my relationship with my husband? Am I interceding for my husband on a daily basis?

<u>Pray Together</u>: Our Heavenly Father, help us to be submitted first to you, then to one another in mutual submission. Help us to press forward toward the prize for your glory, and for the Kingdom!

#96 FREEDOM

"It is for freedom that Christ has set us free." —Galatians 5:1

Freedom is a wonderful thing—if we understand what it means. Whether we speak of national freedom or personal freedom the principles are the same. Today, we are seeing a national decline of civility and order impacting our marriages and families. As the Church goes, so goes the family; as the family goes, so goes the nation. Freedom is never absolute. It is bounded by the will and purposes of God. Freedom is to know that I am personally accepted and loved by the Supreme Judge of the universe, therefore, I'm not in need of the approval of others. I am free to be who God made me to be, fully and completely. We hold ourselves accountable to God and His laws as we come to know, and accept one another for who we are. Freedom is knowing that I am free to pass on to my children a legacy of faith, hope and love. The next generation will be deeply impacted by choices we make—or fail to make—even as we are deeply impacted by the choices our parents made.

Ultimate freedom is the freedom to follow Christ. Outside of Christ there is only bondage, seen or unseen, which results in misery in this life, and an eternity separated from the God who made us. It is for freedom that Christ has set us free. Therefore let us freely pursue His will, and the joy promised will be more than just words in a book. It will be real in our lives, in our marriage, in our family and in our nation.

<u>*Question for Dialogue:*</u> Do we really value and exercise our freedoms to be the very best we can, or are we still in bondage to people, circumstances, or attitudes?

<u>*Pray Together:*</u> Lord, help us to know the freedom that sets us free to soar to new heights in love, mercy, and yes, even righteousness.

#97 Oh Holy Vacation

> *"Six days do your work, but on the seventh day do not work, so that your ox and your donkey may rest and the slave born in your household, and the alien as well, may be refreshed."*
> —Exodus 23:12

I remember when I used to feel guilty if I took time off for vacation, especially during those early years, planting a church, or shepherding a congregation. There was always so much work to do! Our society seems to place such a high value on "busy-ness." Throughout Scripture the Sabbath principle reminds us that it is nothing less than God's instruction to take time on a regular basis to rest and be renewed and re-energized in order to serve God, and others more effectively. It happens to us too. We spend so much time helping others with their marriages that, we too, need time just to enjoy each other, to rest in one another's arms without having to think of the things that need to be done, or the people who need to be called, or the bills that need to be paid. Make a "holiday" (Which derives from the words "holy day") a priority for your marriage. Be sure to schedule time to go to the beach or a quiet lake for an entire week if you can. Be renewed in every way so you can better serve God in the way you love and treat each other, and those who look to you to see what love is supposed to look like.

Question for Dialogue: Do we really take enough time on a regular basis to enjoy one another, and to be renewed and refreshed so that we can serve God and others more effectively?

Pray Together: Lord, help us to make the time we need to enjoy this gift of marriage. Help us to have a "holy-day" worth singing about.

#98 What are Vacations For?

> *"Love the LORD your God with all your heart and with all your soul and with all your strength."* —Deuteronomy 6:5

Summer vacations, a time to re-connect, rediscover, and rededicate. First we need to reconnect with our Maker. Get out in the woods, on the lake, ponder the mighty seas, but gaze on His magnificent creation and look for the hands and the heart that have created such beauty. And say again, *"I will love the Lord with all my heart, and all my soul and all my strength."* That means He's Number One. He won't take second place. If He isn't Lord of all, He's not Lord at all. He won't play second fiddle. Secondly, rediscover God's will for you. Get into His Word like never before. Now that the children are home, use this time to teach the children, not just in a formal family devotional setting, but when you're with them on the beach. Tell them how God promised Abraham that his descendants would be as the grains of sand on the shore. If you're not sure where to look, and you're in the woods, look up "trees" and you can teach your children how the "trees" of the fields clap their hands in praise of God, and how the mountains will "bow down" and the seas will "roar" at the sound of His name. There's so much that a good family vacation can tell about our God. Then let's rededicate ourselves as a family, first to God, then to one another. It's up to Dad to provide that loving leadership (No tyrants allowed). We can gather and thank God for this time of refreshing and rest, and rededicate ourselves to Him, and His purposes for our lives. Let's commit our home to being a place where "each lives for the other, and all live for God." Let's re-connect, re-discover and re-dedicate. That will be the best part of our whole vacation.

Question for Dialogue: How can we schedule a vacation, and include God in our plans?

Pray Together: Lord, help us to have a time of rest and refreshing where we can reconnect with you, rediscover your will for our marriage and family, and rededicate our family to your purposes.

Fall

*"Be patient, then, brothers and sisters,
until the Lord's coming.
See how the farmer waits for the land
to yield its valuable crop,
patiently waiting for the
autumn and spring rains".*
—James 5:7

#99 Changing Seasons

> *"He changes times and seasons; he removes kings and sets up kings; he gives wisdom to the wise and knowledge to those who have understanding;"* —Daniel 2:21

The trees are shedding their leaves—finally! The air is cool and crisp. Another season of change. I believe with all my heart that this is a time to re-order our lives. God first, the marriage second, the children third and everything else follows. We must endeavor to build relationships, especially in our families. In this fast and furious digital culture we've forgotten how to have relationships. Many are too busy working to provide for their families while sacrificing relationships. What kind of sense does that make? What does the worker gain from his toil? Is he but chasing after the wind? Let's stop acting like mindless gerbils running aimlessly in a cage that spins but goes nowhere. It's time for change! Time to reorder our lives for positive change. Let's make those needed changes in our priorities, in our schedules, in our vision and goals. (You do have a vision, don't you?) Write them down. Where do we want to be spiritually, in our marriage, in our family, in our careers, six months from now, a year from now, five years from now? There will be change. That you can't avoid. But whether those changes move us toward greater love, peace and joy will be determined by our willingness to exercise the mind God gave us to understand the times, remembering always to keep an eye on that eternity which God has already set in our hearts.

Question for Dialogue: What's changing in our lives? How are things different than they were last year at this time? What changes in priorities and schedules do we have to make?

Pray Together: Lord, help us to re-order our lives putting You first, our marriage second, our children third, then everything else. Help us be prepared to enter into eternity when you call. It could be today.

#100 For Him (Election Day)

"For through the law I died to the law so that I might live for God." —Galatians 2:19

I just called a pastor friend to congratulate him on a letter to the editor he wrote about the injustices of divorce laws in New York. It was not only published in the New York Times, but it was also re-published in a book, "Cutting the Divorce Rate in Half" by Mike McManus. My friend was surprised to hear it was actually in a book, to be read by thousands, and become part of the recorded history of the marriage restoration movement in the U.S. You see, my pastor friend realizes this is not just about him, or even his marriage –*It's about the Kingdom of God!* This Tuesday, we'll participate in the most consequential elections of our time. The outcome will determine whether this nation will remain one nation "under God" for another generation, or whether we will go the way of other nations that abandoned the Lordship of Christ to be driven by godless self-interests. Like my pastor friend realized –and like we must realize—*it's not about us!* It's much bigger. Whether we live or die, whether our marriage is saved or not, we must be obedient to reflect the nature and character of Christ. We must vote for godly leadership in our nation, and we must demonstrate godly leadership in our homes, and His Kingdom will advance in ways beyond what we can imagine. Just think; we get to be part of it as we live for God, *and not for us!*

<u>Question for Dialogue</u>: Do we fulfill our responsibility as Christian Americans to vote on Election Day? Who will we vote for?

<u>Pray Together</u>: Lord, help us to make a difference this Election Day so that we will pass on to our children the same liberty our parents passed on to us.

#101 A Grateful Heart

"Therefore since we are receiving a kingdom that cannot be shaken, let us be thankful, and so worship God acceptably with reverence and awe, for our God is a consuming fire"
—Hebrews 12:28

With all the current gloomy news reports these days, it's important to focus on the blessings of God, and the goodness He has provided with the gift of marriage, and the spouse he has given us. Not only will this make us feel better, but it is also a basic principle of our faith. In fact, having a grateful heart is an act of worship. It's not what you do, but rather who you are. It's about your heart condition. Is gratitude filling your heart for the spouse God gave you? If it is, it should be overflowing so your spouse will see and hear and feel the love of God flowing through. If it isn't there, go before the throne, fall on your face before Him in reverence and awe, and ask for a new heart, for God is a consuming fire and He will not be mocked. He will do the surgery without anesthetic. It will be painful, but it will be so worth it. After the surgery comes the spiritual therapy – exercising your faith by counting your blessings until your heart of gratitude muscle has overcome your grumbling muscle. Then you'll be worshiping Him in spirit and in truth as you are both submitted to one another out of reverence for Christ. That's when it all comes together! And it's so good!

Question for Dialogue: Is gratitude the primary attitude of my heart? Does it show in the way we treat each other?

Pray Together: Lord please do the heart surgery if you must. Grant us hearts of Thanksgiving for all that you have given us, especially our salvation, our marriage and our family.

#102 Thanksgiving – It's Fundamental

"Enter his gates with thanksgiving; go into his courts with praise. Give thanks to him and praise his name"
—Psalm 100:4

The Psalmist says we enter his gates with thanksgiving. In other words, we can't even enter into God's presence without a grateful heart. There are just two kinds of people in the world: the grateful and the grumblers. The grateful understand that everything they have is by God's grace. We have a right to nothing but Hell, for the wages of sin are death. (Romans 3:23) The only thing our good deeds have earned for us is an eternity where the fire is not quenched and the worm does not die. So, every morning when I awake to discover I'm not in Hell I have something to be thankful for. Everything else is a bonus! The grumbler is the one who thinks he deserves something more than Hell. He even thinks he has a right to be –dare I say it-—*happy!* The grumbler cannot enter into God's presence because he is separated by a heart condition that keeps him separated from God and others. Who wants to hang around grumblers, except other grumblers? A thankful heart is fundamental to any relationship, whether with God, your spouse or anyone else. We must first think, and know in our hearts when we try to relate with each other, "I thank God for His grace in my life, and you are part of it." Only when that foundation is laid can we begin to enjoy relationship with God, and with one another. What's the alternative? Living a life of grumbling here to be followed by an eternity in Hell? I'd rather be grateful. No matter what my circumstances, they are better than what I deserve, and I will be forever entering into His gates with Thanksgiving in my heart. Let's do it!

<u>*Question for Dialogue*</u>: Do you think I'm grateful or am I a grumbler?

<u>*Pray Together*</u>: Lord, give us hearts of Thanksgiving for every good gift we have. It's all so much more than what we deserve; it's your grace!

LOVE IS...

We've all seen the little cartoons in the newspapers entitled, *"Love is..."* Thousands of different cartoons are illustrated suggesting the idea that love is really so many things, a great mystery, and so we can only illustrate what it may suggest.

Well, love is no mystery. In fact, all we have to do is to look to the Cross, and there we see love in all its fullness. Love is sacrificing for the needs of another, as Christ demonstrated by sacrificing Himself for our need of salvation.

The Bible gives us a clear definition of love. Here, in this next section we'll look at 1 Corinthians 13:4-7, (You know, that verse that we often hear recited at weddings.) We'll examine each characteristic of love and see how it may be working—or not working—in our own marriage.

We will learn to love with God's help.

After all, that's what the sum total of our Christian faith is all about, it's about one thing; it's about *Learning to Love!*

#103 Love Is Patient

"Love is patient..." — 1 Corinthians 13:4

Sometimes the King James' version says it best. It translates patience as "long suffering." And what does long-suffering mean? Suffering long! That's it! "But I've suffered long enough." you say. Oh, have you? Look at the palms of your hands. See any nail scars there yet? Then you haven't suffered as much as Christ has suffered for you. Put another way; you haven't been as patient with others as Christ has been with you. He is patient with us, and continues to accept us and love us for who we are, not what we are. He continues to forgive us even while we're in the act of sin as long as our hearts are really turned toward Him, and we truly desire to do His will. Husbands and wives are both struggling to change daily. The key is to be patient with one another as we are both struggling. Let's be encouraging for whatever progress we see, and not become impatient because we're not seeing more. It will come. Don't push it. Enjoy the ride. Paul tells us we need two things to see all that God has reserved for us: faith and patience, (Hebrews 6:12). When we blow it, it's usually because we don't have the faith or patience to persevere. We're just not willing to suffer long enough to see the breakthrough. Be patient with one another, forgiving one another, just as God, in Christ Jesus forgave you. Love is patient. To the extent that we are patient we are loving. To the extent that we are not, we are not loving. That's the truth!

Question for Dialogue: How have we been impatient with one another? How does it affect our relationship and the atmosphere in our home?

Pray Together: Lord, help us to remember how you are longsuffering-with us, so that we may have patience for one another, and through faith and patience realize the promises you have made us.

#104 LOVE IS KIND

"Love is patient, love is kind. ....." —1 Corinthians 13:4

What is "kind"? I mean, it's a nice sounding word, but where can we see it in real life, particularly in this fast paced society where everyone is busy expressing their anger and demanding their rights? After all, when was the last time you even heard the word "kind" on a TV sitcom other than when someone tried to decide what "kind" of pizza to send out for. Unfortunately, kindness is not exactly in vogue in our culture, but it's absolutely essential for a healthy loving relationship. So we need to swim against the modern currents to do what Paul tells us: "...be tenderhearted and kind." Kindness can best be seen and heard in our tone of voice. Is there a tender heart behind the way we address one another? Or, is there gruffness and hardness? Do we sound annoyed, angry or frustrated? If that's the case, we need to choose to be tenderhearted and kind. We need to replace our gruffness with softness, our insensitivity with tenderness. One way to do this is to think about your spouse, "I love you" before you speak. Just bringing that truth to mind will change your countenance and the very spirit behind your words. It's easy to be angry, frustrated or annoyed. That's natural. Let's choose to do what's unnatural: be tenderhearted and kind. To the extent that we are being kind, we are loving. To the extent that we aren't being kind, we are not loving. That's the plain and simple truth

Question for Dialogue: "When do we find it most difficult to be tenderhearted and kind to one another? How can we work on reminding ourselves to be gentle, soft, tenderhearted and kind?

Pray Together: Lord, help us to be tenderhearted and kind with one another. Remind us to think, "I love you," before we speak. Help us to model that tenderhearted and kind demeanor for our children.

#105 Love Does Not Envy

"... love is kind. It does not envy," —1 Corinthians 13:4

I remember my days as a younger preacher, how I would look at T.V. evangelists with their large followings, and think to myself, "Someday..." I thought it was all right to pastor a "small" church, as long as it would lead to getting a much larger ministry down the road. By envying others, and coveting what I didn't have, I truly missed out on the joy of knowing what I did have. That's the problem with envy. It distracts you from enjoying what you have by getting you to fantasize over what you don't have. Envy will not only steal your joy, but it will turn it into grumbling, and eventually, into anger. You will begin to believe that you actually deserve more than what you have, and circumstances, or maybe other people, are keeping you from what you think you deserve. You will come to resent others or your circumstances. You'll be miserable. Envy keeps us from knowing the joy of the now, the God of the now. Today, when our family sits around the table for dinner, and the conversation gets downright hilarious, I often become overwhelmed with joy, thinking of the love that we have in our home. We have no big T.V. ministry, no big church, no big home or fancy car, but what we have is love. What joy! There's no sense of envy. I already have more than what I deserve. Why miss the joy of the now? Life is too short. Thank God I don't have what I deserve, or I'd be burning in hell about now. As Paul said, "I have learned to be content in whatever state I'm in." It took me a while to learn that lesson. It's my prayer for you that you'll be just a little quicker to learn than I was.

Question for Dialogue: What are some of the things we find ourselves coveting? Who do we envy, and why?

Pray Together: Lord, help us to focus on the now, and to be grateful for what we have, instead of envying others. Help us to realize that if all we have is Jesus, we already have more than we deserve.

#106 LOVE DOES NOT BOAST!

"...Love is kind...it does not boast..." — 1 Corinthians 13:4

Nothing turns me off more than someone blowing their own horn trying to convince the world that they are so great and wonderful. Most of us can recognize that behavior in social settings pretty easily, but in marriage, boasting takes a more subtle nature, but it's just as repulsive. Real love doesn't look to promote itself, because it's too busy looking to promote others. The two are mutually exclusive. You can't build up others while you're building up yourself. Leave that up to God. He can do a much better job than you can. He wants to build you up to others, but you have to let Him do it by getting out of the way. Get out of self-promotion, or even self-defending, and get into promoting your spouse, defending your spouse. Be the president of your spouses' fan club, the captain of their cheerleading team. Choose to walk in humility, a choice that says I will not defend myself, promote myself, or try to lift myself above any other. I will leave that up to God. Instead, I will give my life to promoting others, to building them up in any way I can. Nobody loves a braggart, or one who is promoting or defending themselves. Leave that up to God, and choose to be one who will give your life to bragging on others, promoting others, defending others, the first of which will be your spouse, and believe me, God will take care of bragging on you.

Question for Dialogue: When do I feel that you tend to brag or boast about yourself in ways that cause me to feel negatively toward you?

Pray Together: Lord, help us to focus on lifting up each other, instead of promoting, bragging, or even defending ourselves. Help us to be each other's number one cheerleader, and to trust you for our own promotion."

#107 Love Is Not Proud

"Love is patient…it is not proud…" -1 Corinthians 13:4

Love is not proud? What does that mean? Often we think of pridefulness, as someone "struttin' their stuff," or thinking of themselves as being better than others in very visible ways. Here is a definition that will change your idea of pride forever, if you'll take hold of it. Ready? Here it goes:

Pride isn't thinking too much of yourself; it's thinking of yourself too much!

That's right. It's possible to be prideful even while you're putting yourself down, saying, "Woe is me. I'm just not worthy, just not good enough." Your focus is still on yourself! You're focused on yourself just as much as the person who thinks too highly of himself or herself. You're still thinking of yourself! You can't be thinking of another person's well-being; you're too self-focused. That's pride! Never mind you're unworthiness. God doesn't make junk. You're worthy because He makes you worthy. And guess what? You're no better than the next guy. You have nothing that God didn't give you, and nothing He can't take back in a moment. So you have nothing to focus on about yourself, either thinking too highly of yourself, or thinking too lowly of yourself. Quit thinking about yourself. It's not about you! Love is not proud. It doesn't focus on self. It focuses on God, and the wellbeing of others.

<u>Question for Dialogue:</u> What are some of the ways you think I may be too self-conscious? Does my pridefulness show up when I'm thinking too highly of myself, or when I'm thinking too lowly of myself?

<u>Pray Together</u>: Lord, help us not to think of ourselves too much, either too highly, or too lowly. Help us to be focused on you first, then each other. Forgive our pridefulness. Replace it with humility, focusing on the wellbeing of others first."

#108 Love Is Not Rude

"Love is patient...It is not rude..." -1 Corinthians 13:4,5

The word "rude" suggests something rough, unpolished or unfinished. Love is not rude because it is not rough, unpolished, or unfinished. Love is perfect because God is love, and God is perfect. We, human beings, are the ones who are often rough, unpolished, and unfinished. To the extent that we demonstrate rudeness we demonstrate just how rough, or immature, we really are. Rudeness is exactly that: immaturity, and undeveloped character. As a person grows, and matures, as they become fashioned over time by the hand of their Creator, they learn how to use self-control to be a blessing to others. They learn how to prefer others above themselves. They learn how to be more concerned with the other person's feelings rather than their own. Rudeness is evidence of self-centered undeveloped character. I don't care how long you've called yourself a Christian, the bottom line is, if you're still rude to each other, to your children, or to anyone else, you are still self-centered, rough, unpolished and undeveloped as a person created in God's image. Love is not rude because love is complete, finished, polished! True love can only really be shared by grown-ups.

Question for Dialogue: How grown-up are we when we measure ourselves by how rude we are to one another? When do we tend to fall into rudeness?

Pray Together: Lord, help us to grow up, spiritually, and emotionally, just as we have intellectually and physically. Help us to be not rough, but finished and polished by your own hand.

#109 Love Is Not Self-Seeking

"Love is patient..., it is not self-seeking..." — 1 Corinthians 13:5

It seems like ever since the 1960's, Americans have been on some quest to find themselves. Over fifty years later the fruit of our labors is evident: People are more lost, more confused, more clueless than ever. This hip idea was obviously a loser. Secular therapists who haven't found themselves yet, are helping more people get more lost every day. Jesus gave us the answer two thousand years ago, (but of course, we're too sophisticated to believe a carpenter's son who has no letters after his name.) Basically, He said, "If you really want to find yourself, lose yourself, then you'll find yourself." (My paraphrase) Give yourself to serving others, and your own needs and desires will be met. Give yourself to serving your spouses' needs. Be a blessing, not a source of tension. Forget about yourself, your wants, your needs or even your rights. The only thing we have a right to is an eternity in hell for our sin, "where the fire is not quenched and the worm does not die!" Thank God He doesn't treat us according to our rights. But instead, Jesus saw our need. He didn't seek His own will. He was fully human, and as such, really didn't want to go the cross, but He concluded, "...nevertheless, not my will be done but thine," and He went. Then God raised Him from the dead and gave Him total victory. That's the way it works. Forget about yourself. Give yourself for others, and then God will give you the victory that you've been fighting so hard to get on your own. Love is being a God-seeker, not a self-seeker. Live to serve God, your spouse and your family, and you will have it all —promise!

Question for Dialogue: Do you think I am self-seeking? Can you think of some examples?

Pray Together: Lord, help us to be surrendered to Jesus, denying ourselves and our selfish desires for a greater cause. Help us to be God-seekers, not self-seekers.

#110 Love Is Not Easily Angered

Love is patient...it is not easily angered — 1 Corinthians 13:5

Anger is not, in itself a bad thing. Jesus was angry at the temple when he turned the tables of the moneychangers, yet He was without sin. Scripture tell us: "Be angry and sin not,"(Ephesians 4:26). So anger isn't the problem. It's the object and the expression of that anger that gets us into trouble. If we are easily angered the problem may be that we aren't just a person who gets angry, but we are an angry person. There's a difference. An angry person is filled with anger because of some perceived injustice, which they believe in their hearts, was perpetrated on them; sometimes it was something that took place years ago. Because they haven't been able to resolve that sense of injustice they carry it with them, and it lurks just under the surface waiting to be triggered by the slightest provocation. These people become unapproachable and incapable of having a healthy relationship. If you are an angry person you do not have the ability to love. It's impossible. If you want to love you need to resolve the anger issue. Identify it. Bring it into the light where the blood of Jesus is to bring forgiveness, healing, cleansing and new hope, (1 John 1:7,8). Only then, can you begin to receive God's love for yourself and for others. Until then, you will remain an angry, and an emotionally handicapped person. If you can honestly say you aren't an angry person, but you do get easily angered, then check your expectations. Either others aren't giving what you expect, or they are giving what you don't expect. Your expectations need to be readjusted.

Question for Dialogue: Are we easily angered? Are we approachable? Are we people who get angry, or are we angry people? Where do we need to adjust our expectations?

Pray Together: Lord, help us to resolve our anger issues so that we may be capable of having a loving relationship. Bring into the light any hidden source of anger so that we may deal with it and move forward.

#111 Love Keeps No Record of Wrongs

"Love is patient...It keeps no record of wrongs."
— 1 Corinthians 13:5

Do you sometimes feel like your spouse has a file cabinet hidden away somewhere with files filled with all the things you did wrong in all your years of marriage? Whenever you have an argument, or you do something wrong, out comes that list of offenses — half of which you already forgot? How will you ever live down the past? There's nothing you can do about it. You can change now, but if you mess up, out comes that list of past offenses. How could he or she remember them the way they do? It seems like they have them stored somewhere just waiting for you to mess up, doesn't it? Well, guess what — *they do!* These offenses are all recorded in the brain. If you could open up your spouses' head and look inside — yours too for that matter — you'll find a file cabinet in there with a bunch of folders, listed with each offense you committed since you first met. It is a record of wrongs. Whenever you mess up out comes the appropriate folder with a whole set of similar offenses to prove you're a serial offender. "You'll never change!" As long as that file cabinet exists you're sunk. Forget it. Guilty! The only way we can really change is to burn up those files and throw out the file cabinet. Then there will be no record of wrongs to keep bringing us back when we want to move forward as a new creation. Love is burning the files and throwing out the file cabinet. Hold no record of wrongs.

<u>Question for Dialogue</u>: Does it really seem like we have a file cabinet in our minds that provides us ammunition to accuse one another of our hurtful past?

<u>Pray Together:</u> Lord, Help us to burn up the old files and throw out the file cabinet in our minds. Help us to hold no record of wrongs against one another. Help us to walk in newness of life every morning.

#112 Love Doesn't Delight In Evil

"Love does not delight in evil..." —1 Corinthians 13:6a

We don't usually think of ourselves as people who would delight in evil, but think about the last time you quietly gloated over someone else's misfortune, or just thought to yourself, "Gee, I'm glad it's not me." Did you delight in the fact that it was someone else's tough luck? When your husband or wife made a mistake, and had to suffer the consequences of that mistake, were you supportive, or did the look on your face say, "I told you so!"? Love doesn't delight in evil. Love mourns over evil. It is saddened by sin. Love doesn't gloat. It hurts with the hurts of others. Imagine a person falling into a ditch. Finding himself at the bottom, he looks up, and there sees a friend looking down on him. Then the friend says, "Hey Stupid, how did you fall into that ditch? Were you drunk or something? Just climb out. It can't be that hard. I told you not to hang around open ditches anyway?" Then you see Jesus. He doesn't say a word. He just climbs down into the ditch, comes alongside the person and gently helps him up until he's safely out. Jesus is our model. Let's not gloat over our spouses' misfortunes, or rejoice that it's not us, or be quick to pass judgment. Let's simply get go down into the ditch-that's compassion- and gently help each other to recover and find healing. Let's be Jesus to one another.

Question for Dialogue: Do I feel supported by you when I fall, or do I feel like you gloat, or are quick to judge me? Do I feel that you delight when I make a mistake?

Pray Together: Lord, help us to be sensitive to one another's hurts. Help us to remember that we need to make it together. Help us not to delight in seeing each other fall, but help us to be a "lifter upper" not a "put downer."

#113 Rejoices With Truth

"Love doesn't delight in evil but rejoices with truth."
—1 Corinthians 13:6

Isn't it interesting how Paul doesn't contrast evil with good in this passage, but instead, he contrasts it with truth. On the one hand you have evil, and on the other, you have not good, but truth! That's because truth is good! "But the truth of my situation isn't so good," you might say. I hear you. But let's first understand that no matter what your situation looks like, you're only seeing part of it. The truth of it goes beyond what you see. Truth has a Name; it's Jesus! He said, "I am the Way, the Truth, and the Life" (John 14:6) Jesus is the truth of your situation. And to the extent that your situation is in His hands it's good, regardless of what you see! Please don't be one of those weird, normal people (talk about an oxymoron!) who are limited by physical reality. The Truth is that no matter what you see, Jesus really is able to bring it to a good report. He really is able to do the impossible, to take our mess, and do something beautiful with it —if we'll only let him. That's why no matter where we are, we can rejoice with the Truth —with Jesus! Love stays focused, not on our situation but on Jesus. He is the one who is able to do what we can't, who can provide what we need, who can lift us up when we're down, who can give us the love we need for each other—a love we just don't have in the natural. The truth is that we can do all things through Christ who strengthens us. Rejoice!!

Question for Dialogue: What is the truth of our marriage? What has God promised us that He will do if we will let Him?

Pray Together: Lord helps us to not focus on the problems in our marriage, but on the Truth of your promises. Help us to rejoice in that truth as we see it come to pass.

#114 Love Always Protects

"Love is patient... It always protects" —1 Corinthians 13:7

If love always protects, and I love my spouse, then it ought to be true that I always protect my spouse. Not only when she (he) is in physical danger—that's understood—but also from the danger of emotional injury as well. When others say something derogatory about my wife do I just "let it slide" or do I protect her so that others will know they dare not say one negative word about my wife in my presence? Do I protect her from hurtful words of others? Do I protect her from my own hurtful words? Am I approachable? Is it emotionally safe to talk about anything with me, or is it a matter of "walking on eggshells"?

Let's be honest. Could it be that I am the greatest source of emotional hurt in my spouses' life? If that's the case, then I guess I don't have a clue about what real love is—a love that always, always protects. If I'm not protecting her from my own hurtful words, then I'm really not loving my wife, regardless of what I would like to think. That's the gospel truth—the bottom line.

Question for Dialogue: How do we feel protected by one another? How do we feel unprotected? Do we feel unprotected by each other?

Pray Together: Lord, help us to protect one another against hurtful words of others, unhealthy situations, and above all, help us to protect each other from ourselves. Help us to always, always, protect.

#115 LOVE ALWAYS TRUSTS

"Love is patient... It always protects, always trusts..."
—1 Corinthians 13:7

Love always trusts. Boy, that's a tough one! How can I trust my spouse after I've been hurt so much? Why should I trust when I see no reason to think he or she will ever change, or even wants to change? Won't I just be setting myself up for more hurt and disappointment? Those are some pretty valid questions, and truth be told, most of us aren't really trustworthy anyway. To put your trust in a spouse who isn't trustworthy makes no sense. You will be hurt again, and become more bitter and angry. Your condition will be worse in the end then it was in the beginning. God isn't calling you to put your trust in a person who is unable or unwilling to honor that trust. Then what does the word mean when it says "love always trusts"? It simply means that when I can't trust my spouse, I can trust God for my spouse. It may mean pressing into God as never before. You can't trust someone you don't know, even if it is God. You must press into God until you know how trustworthy He really is. This only comes by worship, prayer and reading His Word. Develop an intimate and personal relationship with God so that you can trust Him to keep your spouse, and to be working in your spouses' heart and mind. Know Him so that you can trust He is working in both of you to give you a marriage He can display to the world as His handiwork. Love always trusts. You can love, because you can always trust, if not in your spouse, then in the God who is watching over your spouse.

Question for Dialogue: What areas do I feel I can trust you for? What areas do I feel I can only trust God for?

Pray Together: Lord help us to develop a trust in you that is greater than all our fears and anxieties, knowing that as we grow in trust in you for our marriage, we will also grow in a healthy trust in one another.

#116 Love Always Hopes

"It always protects, always trusts, always hopes…"
— 1 Corinthians 13:7

The writer of Hebrews tells us that we have this hope, (the hope of His promises) as an anchor for the soul, (Hebrews 6:19a). We all need to be anchored in a firm and secure truth that will keep us steady through the uncertain times and stormy seasons in our relationships. Otherwise, we may find ourselves adrift in a sea of confusion, discouragement and aimlessness. If we let go of the dream we had when we said, "I do" we may find ourselves tossed on the seas of uncertainty and insecurity with an overriding fear that we may find ourselves one day washed up on a desert island all alone. But love always hopes. It's always anchored in the promises of God, the promises we believed when we said "I do." That is our anchor. That's what will keep us steady and focused, not on the stormy seas, but on the calm beyond the horizon. God's promises are still good. That's why we can hope, and why that hope will not disappoint us if we will persevere. No matter how long the stormy night, the sun will still rise, and God's promises are still good. That is the anchor for my soul. That's why real love always hopes.

Question for Dialogue: What were the hopes and dreams we had when we were first married? What will our marriage and family look like when these hopes become reality?

Pray Together: Lord, help us to continue to stay anchored and unmoved in our faith to see your promises become reality. Help us to continue to place our hopes in your faithful promises.

#117 LOVE ALWAYS PERSEVERES

"Love always protects... it always perseveres"
—1 Corinthians 13:7

The world's ways are abort, divorce and cop out. God's ways are commit, submit and don't quit. This formula is the key to success whether we're talking about business or relationships. I can't tell you how often I felt like quitting when things got rough between Penny and myself. But we had closed the back door in our minds. There was no way out. Divorce wasn't an option. First we had to commit to the goal of achieving the marriage we both knew God wanted us to have. Then we had to submit to doing whatever it would take to see that happen. That was tough for me. I'm not very good at submitting to anything, or anybody. I guess I had a problem with that typical guy thing –pride. Ultimately, I had to accept the fact that God did know more than me. His ways were better than mine. How do you like that? Then it was a matter of persevering; working through the issues, trying to communicate, getting angry, asking forgiveness, then doing it all over again, and again and again. It was tough, but we didn't give up. We didn't cop out. We didn't divorce. By our choice and God's power we persevered, and God brought us through. That's one trip I never want to go on again. But what we have now was worth all the work, strain and pain we went through. We have love, real honest-to-goodness love for each other, freely and willingly given. It's great! But we never would have seen it had we quit. Thank God we didn't. Persevere. Commit, submit and don't quit. It works!

Question for Dialogue: When do I feel like I want to quit? When do I feel you want to quit?

Pray Together: Lord, give us the power to persevere, to commit to the marriage, to submit to do whatever it takes, then to stick to it until we see the fulfillment of your promise to bring restoration, righteousness, peace and joy.

#118 Love Never Fails

"...Love never fails" — 1 Corinthians 13:8

Today, Penny and I can look back over our fifty years of marriage, all the trials we've been through, all the difficulties we've had with each other, with finances, with children; It's been a long tough road, but has it been worth it? Let me share with you a card Penny just sent me. (She sends me cards even though we work together in the same office. The personal stuff she wrote, I'll keep personal):

"I wish we could run away, find some little uninhabited island, And just make love to each other day and night for the rest of our lives... I know that's selfish, but sometimes the pressures and responsibilities of daily life leave us so little time and energy for spending time together, And in my mind, that's the most important thing of all. I love you so very much! So please don't ever think for a moment that you're not my first priority, because no matter where I am, or what I'm doing, in my heart, I'm on that little island with you, loving you until the end of time."

When I eventually got my composure back after reading that (Who said big men don't cry?) I realized the truth of God's word, "Love never ...never...never...fails!" For all that we've been through, for all that we've never acquired or accomplished, we have seen the fulfillment of God's promise: *We have love!* All the worldly success couldn't buy what Jesus bought for us on the cross—the ability to love with his unconditional, limitless love, a love that truly never fails.

<u>**Question for Dialogue**</u>: How have we seen God's love come through for us over the years?

<u>**Pray Together:**</u> Lord, help us to continue to walk in your unconditional love for one another with the knowledge in our hearts that your love will never fail us.

Prayer For Our Marriage

Father, marriage was your idea. It is one of your divinely created institutions. We have entered into this covenant freely, and do hereby commit ourselves to do whatever it takes to be good stewards of this covenant. We confess our sinfulness and self-centered ways and choose to do your will. It is written in Your Word that love is shed abroad in our hearts by the Holy Spirit who is given to us. Because You are in us, we acknowledge that love reigns supreme. We believe that love is displayed in full expression enfolding and knitting us together in truth, making us perfect for every good work to do Your will and working in us that which is pleasing in Your sight.

We live and conduct ourselves, and our marriage honorably and becomingly. We esteem it as precious, worthy and of great price. We commit ourselves to live in mutual harmony and accord with one another delighting in each other, being of the same mind and united in spirit.

Father, we believe and say that we are gentle, compassionate, courteous, tender-hearted and humble-minded. We seek peace and it keeps our hearts in quietness and assurance. Because we are committed to learning to love and dwell in peace, our prayers are not hindered in any way. We are heirs together of the grace of God in Jesus Christ.

Our marriage grows stronger day by day in the bond of unity because it is founded on Your Word and rooted and grounded in Your love. Father, we thank You for the performance of it, in Jesus' name:'-Amen!

TO BE A CHRISTIAN

To be a Christian is not a matter of formal religion, but a matter of personal relationship with Jesus Christ. One of the reasons why marriage was given to us was to provide an example of what our relationship with Jesus Christ should be.

When we said "I do" it spoke of a life-long commitment to another person, to give that person number one place in our hearts. Well, to be a Christian means to say "I do" to Jesus Christ, and give Him that number one place. A Christian, quite simply, is a person who has placed Jesus Christ in that very special place in their hearts—number one! You can know if you are a Christian and have the assurance of eternal life by simply looking into your own heart and asking, "Who's number one there?" If it's yourself, another person, your job or even a formal religion you do not have the promise of salvation. It's time to dethrone that idol and place Jesus Christ in His rightful place. You can say a simple prayer like this, but be sure it comes from the heart.

Dear Heavenly Father,

I confess that you have not been number one in my life. I'm sorry. Please forgive me. Jesus, come into my life; cleanse me of my sin and take your rightful place on the throne of my life. No longer will I ask you to bless me so I can live my life the way I want. From this day forward I seek your plan for my life and will try to live according to your Word. Give me the wisdom to know your will and the power—by your Holy Spirit—to do it.

Thank you, Jesus, for hearing my prayer. Thank you for dying on the cross to pay the penalty for my sin. Thank you for my new and everlasting life.—Amen.

If you have prayed this prayer please drop us an email and let us know. It's most important that you find a Bible-believing church and begin to grow. This is only the beginning of an exciting and wonderful journey into the fullness of His love. In fact, you can't really know love until you know God.

Our Marriage Journal

Our Marriage Journal

Our Marriage Journal

Our Marriage Journal

Our Marriage Journal

Our Marriage Journal

Our Marriage Journal

Our Marriage Journal

Our Marriage Journal

Our Marriage Journal

Our Marriage Journal

TO ORDER MORE BOOKS

You too can be part of the marriage restoration movement.

If you'd like to order more books for family, friends or small group, or if you would like to request that Reverends Bill and Penny come to speak to your church or civic group, just send an email to:

bill@marriageandfamily.org.

Don't forget to visit our website and sign up to receive our latest updates and "Marriage Minutes." Log onto:

www.marriageandfamily.org.

If you have any testimonies, questions or concerns, or would like to know how you can be a part of this ministry just send an email to

info@marriageandfamily.org.

CPSIA information can be obtained
at www.ICGtesting.com
Printed in the USA
BVHW031807190921
617069BV00006B/128